Victor Ojakoro

# Anatomy of the Nig

# African Politics
# Politiques Africaines

## Volume 3

LIT

# Anatomy of the Niger Delta Crisis

## Causes, Consequences and Opportunities for Peace

edited by

Victor Ojakorotu

LIT

**Bibliographic information published by the Deutsche Nationalbibliothek**
The Deutsche Nationalbibliothek lists this publication in the Deutsche Nationalbibliografie; detailed bibliographic data are available in the Internet at http://dnb.d-nb.de.

ISBN 978-3-643-10639-1


A catalogue record for this book is available from the British Library



©LIT VERLAG Dr. W. Hopf Berlin 2010
Fresnostr. 2   D-48159 Münster
Tel. +49 (0) 2 51-620 320   Fax +49 (0) 2 51-922 60 99
e-Mail: lit@lit-verlag.de   http://www.lit-verlag.de

**Distribution:**
In Germany: LIT Verlag Fresnostr. 2, D-48159 Münster
Tel. +49 (0) 2 51-620 32 22, Fax +49 (0) 2 51-922 60 99, e-Mail: vertrieb@lit-verlag.de

In Austria: Medienlogistik Pichler-ÖBZ, e-mail: mlo@medien-logistik.at

In Switzerland: B + M Buch- und Medienvertrieb, e-mail: order@buch-medien.ch

In the UK: Global Book Marketing, e-mail: mo@centralbooks.com

In North America by:

**Transaction Publishers**
New Brunswick (U.S.A.) and London (U.K.)

Transaction Publishers
Rutgers University
35 Berrue Circle
Piscataway, NJ 08854

Phone: +1 (732) 445 - 2280
Fax: + 1 (732) 445 - 3138
for orders (U. S. only):
toll free (888) 999 - 6778
e-mail: orders@transactionpub.com

This book is in memory of my late father, Pa Dickson Omashaye Ojakorotu, and my mother, Mrs Oberhirhi Mary Ojakorotu.

# Contents

i

# Contents

# Acknowledgements

I will like to extend my profound gratitude to Professor Amos Utuama (SAN), and the Delta State Government for supporting the 2008 International Conference on the Niger Delta Crisis, which was hosted in Johannesburg, South Africa: Your generous financial contribution helped make the conference a success.

Also, I wish to express my sincere gratitude to the contributors for the timely submissions of their papers despite tight academic schedules.

In addition, I am indebted to many people, whose support, advice, criticisms and insights made possible the successful completion of this book. I recognise, too, the support that my family gave to me, especially my wife, Ekene, and our little angels, Amaka and Mia: my long absence from home, in order to tidy up this project, never created any doubts in your hearts about my affection for you.

Finally, I would like to thank the following people as well: Professor Adam Simon for his understanding and kind words of encouragements during this academic research; Jamin Ohwovoriole for his editorial service; the research unit of Monash South Africa for its support.

# Contributors

**Mukoro Akpomuvire, Ph.D** is on sabbatical from the Obafemi Awolowo University, Ile-Ife, and he is the current Head of Department of Political Science at the Delta State University, Abraka. Both institutions are in Nigeria. He has written and published major scholarly works in the field of Public Administration in the form of books, chapter contributions to book, articles in both national and international journals, monographs and research findings. Importantly, he is a consultant on Human Resource Management and Governance for the Nigerian federal government, the Delta State government of Nigeria, and several international bodies including the United Nations. He is currently researching the activities of Non-Governmental Organisations, which are involved in Governance in Africa.

**Fidelis Allen** teaches Political Science at the Department of Political and Administrative Studies, University of Port Harcourt, Nigeria. He is a recipient of University for Peace Africa Programme and the 2008 Canadian International Development Research Centre Doctoral Research Award.

**Victor Ojakorotu, Ph.D** obtained his doctorate from the University of the Witwatersrand, Johannesburg, South Africa. He is a lecturer at the Department of International Studies, Monash University, Johannesburg. His primary research interest is in the field of natural resources and conflict in Africa with special focus on the Niger Delta of Nigeria. He has published extensively on the crisis in Nigeria's Niger Delta.

**J. Shola Omotola** lectures at the Department of Political Science and Public Administration, Redeemer's University, Redemption City, Mowe, Ogun State, Nigeria.

**None Morake** is a BA Honours graduate from Monash University in South Africa. The young academic presented an outstanding dissertation, which focused on resource extraction by foreign actors on the African continent, with specific reference to China's role in the Democratic Republic of Congo's copper mining industry. He critiqued the various strategies employed by the People's Republic in acquiring the mineral. His contribution in this book is a reflection of the academic engagement with resource issues in Africa.

**J.S. Oboreh, Ph.D** is of the Department of Business Administration, Delta State University, Abraka, Delta State, Nigeria.

# Contributors

**Henry Alapiki, Ph.D** is the Head of the Department of Political Science, University of Port Harcourt, Choba, Nigeria.

**J.M. Ayuba** is with Nasarawa State University, Keffi, Nigeria.

**Francis George Umukoro, Ph.D** lectures at the Department of Business Administration, Delta State University, Abraka, Delta State, Nigeria

**Matthew I. Eboreime** is of the Department of Economics, Western Delta University, Oghara, Delta State, Nigeria

**Douglason G. Omotor** lectures at the Department of Economics, Delta State University, Abraka, Delta State, Nigeria.

**Franklin A. Sanubi, Ph.D** is a lecturer at the Department of Political Science, Delta State University, Abraka, Nigeria

# 1. Introduction

Dr. Victor Ojakorotu and None Louis Morake

The socio-economic record of Nigeria during the colonial era suggests a flourishing economy that was accompanied by a stable and efficient post-independence African leadership. The immense resource endowments the country possesses with the vast human capital, and the considerable foreign revenue that Nigeria earns provides a blueprint for a thriving independent African state. However, contrary to expectations, the African giant is marred by recurrent political crises, which saw the country engulfed in one crisis or the other. This has resulted in dysfunctional political, economic system of governance that has only benefited a few of the political elite while the masses languish in the midst of resource wealth and distorted resource revenue allocation and distribution. As a result, Nigeria has become synonymous with civil strife, sustained military dictatorships, series of ethno-religious clashes and endemic socio-economic and political conflict since the early 1960s.

Although a democratic administration under the leadership of Olusegun Obasanjo renewed fervour for good governance in 1999, the political economy of the Nigerian state has not experienced any considerable policy shifts, notwithstanding the absence of military rule and authoritarianism. Nigeria has for decades on end stood as sub-Saharan Africa's largest oil exporter, with approximately 2.3 million barrels produced per day. This figure ranks the African state among the world's largest oil producers, only lacking behind Saudi Arabia, Venezuela, Iran, and United Arab Emirates. This oil is extracted in large proportion from the Niger Delta region by foreign multinational companies, and the oil mined in the region accounts for about 80% of Nigeria's revenue.

The dynamics of the crisis in Nigeria, especially in the Niger Delta area, are largely centred on the occurrence of oil, the presence of multinational oil companies that extract the resource, the anti-social and undesirable state policies, the existence of an array of distinct minority ethnic

5

groups as the historical inhabitants of the area, and decisively, the endemic poverty and deficient socio-economic development in spite of the immense resource wealth of the region.

The Niger Delta Crisis has its origins in the colonial era as a result of the unwillingness of the British administration to address the inherent issue of cohabitation between various distinct religious groups and ethnic minorities within a single region. Without dwelling extensively on the role of the colonialists in the making of the Niger Delta Crisis, for the purposes of this book, it is important to highlight the role of successive post-independence government in perpetuating the problematic situation in the region. In addition to neglecting the issue of minorities in policy development and implementation, it can be argued that successive administrations have effectively maintained the historically situated power relations which have undermined the status and ability of ethnic minorities to access the resources in their area.

The development of the Niger Delta Crisis, as it is currently understood, is placed within the historical context of the discovery of large oil reserves in the Bayelsa territory by the oil multinational Shell-BP in 1956. Since this historic occurrence, an account of the Niger Delta revolves around the contestations between the ethnic communities of the region, the multinational oil companies, the federal government as well as various social movements and militias, which have emerged from the state of affairs.

The key areas of contention and underlying causes of the crisis include issues of laws regulating the exploration of oil by multinationals, land ownership, governance, ethnic conflict as well as natural resource control and broader issues of ethnic self-determination of the region's inhabitants. The recurrent violence that has blemished the region, the overall national oil production and issues relating to revenue allocation are a result of the unresolved friction between the series of factors mentioned above.

Since the onset of the crisis, various unsuccessful government-led interventions have been developed; various social groups have formed in protest; youths and disgruntled adults have engaged in widespread violence and organised crime in objection to unfavourable state policies; due international attention has been directed to the predicament of the various groups. Therefore, this book, essentially, addresses the wide-ranging dynamics of the Niger Delta Crisis from a range of detailed perspectives.

In addition to providing the background and context for this book as briefly detailed above, this first chapter aims to provide a summative presentation of each of the chapters that follow. Each chapter is written by an accomplished academic (joint authors in some chapters) from an area of scholastic study and expertise. This equips the writers with ample knowledge, experience and competence to sufficiently address the Niger Delta Crisis with intellectual rigour. By reading through each of the chapters, the reader will be able to engage thoroughly with the academic research conducted by each author, develop a better understanding of how the crisis' dynamics are informed by relevant theoretical approaches, and understand the recommended policy measures that can potentially be employed in future for the resolution of the age-old Niger Delta Crisis.

The second chapter, J.S. Oboreh's "The Origin and the Causes of Crisis in the Niger Delta: the Way Forward", closely examines the origins and causes of the ongoing predicament in the Niger Delta. The author particularly highlights the historical trajectory and development of the crisis while scrutinising the involvement of successive governments as well as foreign oil companies in engendering the enduring misfortune. With regard to the role of the Nigerian government, the author points to the argument that the needs of the people of the Niger Delta have, from a historical standpoint, been highly misunderstood. Oboreh elaborates on the administrative inefficiencies (especially in the definition of the Niger Delta area) and a lack of political will on the part of the (federal) government in relation to the apparent indifference of the state to the people of the Niger Delta. According to the author, notwithstanding the immense financial rewards reaped by the Nigerian government from the extraction of oil, the life in the Niger Delta continues to be characterised by abject poverty, neglect, bad roads, lack of portable drinking water, and general hospitals devoid of drugs, dilapidated school buildings and social frustration. Furthermore, the author notes that the key shortcomings of the Nigerian government, in relation to dealing effectively with the areas of contention involving the Niger Delta, have in the past been compounded by misleading and incomprehensive definition of the Niger Delta region relative to the oil producing states. With regard to the multinational oil companies, Oboreh draws attention to the complicity of these organisations in the exploitation of the resources in the Niger Delta. Coupled with scant concern for environmental conservation and infrastructural development, he argues that the key consequences of the presence of the multinational oil companies in the Niger Delta are the descent of the denizens of the region into enduring poverty and underdevelopment. Finally, the author underscores an array of undesirable economic, political and social consequences of the involvement of the government and the oil companies by pontificating that there is a deep-seated sense of wariness and scepticism amongst the inhabitants of the region due to decades of false promises and misleading developmental programmes initiated by the government and oil companies alike. In conclusion, Oboreh makes several detailed recommendations for the government, including: a representative conference which would give the Niger Delta inhabitants the free-hand to deliberate on key areas of contention such as direct government support for agricultural produce; increased access to finance and capital for business development; concerted action against the rife corruption; and lastly, a special monitoring programme for the appropriate use of oil revenues by the government for the wellbeing of the people of the Niger Delta.

The third chapter, "Oil and Democracy in Nigeria: Oiling the friction?" is written by Henry Alapiki and Fidelis Allen. It diverts attention from the dire consequences of the direct failure of the Nigerian government and the multinational oil companies to pay heed to the welfare and interests of the inhabitants of the Niger Delta. Instead, this chapter provides a meticulous analysis of the mode of extraction and distribution of oil from the Niger Delta by arguing, essentially, that the government's strategies in this regard are fundamentally opposed to democracy. The authors' arguments rest on the assertion that due to the high value of oil on the state's operation and the significant revenues, which can be siphoned from oil extraction, political leaders are willing to extend extreme measures to secure political power. From a historical standpoint, the writers posit that the race by the members of the political elites to access the spoils of the wealth of the Niger Delta is done, many a time, through means which undermine democratic principles. The underlying theme of this chapter is, therefore, premised on the enquiry that oil lubricates the political and socio-economic friction between the Nigerian state and the inhabitants of the Niger Delta, with the key variables being oil, democracy (and federalism), development and friction. To this extent, the authors elaborate on the role of each of the above-mentioned variables in contributing to the unfavourable conditions, which permeate oil extraction and revenue distribution in the Niger Delta.

The fourth chapter addresses the key trends within the Niger Delta Crisis, particularly by tracing the historical context of the quandary. The author, George Umukoro, traces the root cause of the Niger Delta crisis by locating it in the failure of the political elites to address the welfare of the region's populace notwithstanding the significant revenue amassed from the extraction of oil by the state through the multinational oil companies. In addition, the writer employs a thorough theoretical analysis that is based on the dynamics of political theory and the broader implications on underdevelopment of the Niger Delta. This approach, which has not been engaged thoroughly before now, is based on practical research conducted, and it provides a broad range of options for the resolution of the sticky situation in the Niger Delta, ultimately. This chapter argues that there is the need for concerted efforts by relevant stakeholders to address the cycle of poverty in the region; a significant augmentation of the role of the Niger Delta Development Corporation (NDDC) in addressing the needs of the region's communities; the creation of employment opportunities, which must be preceded by the resolution of the perpetual hostility and violence (an outcome which can be attained through the concerted efforts of government agencies in halting the proliferation of small arms and weapons in the region); the effective accomplishment of social responsibility on the part of the various multinational oil companies; collaborative endeavours to properly address the issues of misappropriation and suitable allocation of oil revenues as this is a key area of contention for inhabitants of the region; lastly, the government should actively address the beleaguered educational system since the lack of schooling plays a significant role in the involvement of the youth of the Niger Delta in criminal and violent acts.

Due to the high level of environmental degradation and the various undesirable socio-economic effects that result from intensive resource extraction, the multinational oil companies are deemed to have a direct responsibility to address the welfare of the inhabitants of the Niger Delta. As a result, the fifth chapter addresses the roles of multinational oil companies that operate in the Niger Delta in actively attending to community development imperatives. Authored by Matthew I. Eboreime and Douglason G. Omotor, "Development Interventions of oil Multinationals in Nigeria's Niger

Delta: For the Rich or the Poor" argues that the activities of multinational oil companies have been associated with a range of undesirable environmental concerns, including physical alienation of scarce agricultural land by oil exploration; the flaring of over 70 percent of associated gas, which causes acid rain, reduce soil fertility, pollutes sources of drinking water in addition to recurrent oil spillages, which have been cited as a major cause of decline in agricultural production; and, increase in health problems attributable to oil industry activities. In order to assess the appropriateness of the developmental interventions instituted by the various multinational companies, the authors employ a basic statistical research technique, which also involves a comparative analysis of the role two oil companies, Shell and Agip,have played in the region as both companies jointly produce more than 50 percent of Nigeria's annual crude oil output. The results generally suggests that the developmental measures employed by Shell and Agip did not target the impoverished majority, which are adversely affected by the economic activities of oil companies and are in dire need of socio-economic assistance. Rather, the benefits of the various interventions appear to have had a notably positive impact on the richer segment of the population. In conclusion, the authors recommend that the multinational oil companies operating in the Niger Delta should reassess their development intervention programmes in order to establish new approaches, which may benefit the poorest 30 percent, contrary to the present situation.

The sixth chapter engages with a different dimension of the ongoing Niger Delta Crisis by focusing on the role played by civil society organisations in the imbroglio. Written by Akpomuvire Mukoro, "Governance Failure, Civil Societies and the Niger Delta" begins by phrasing the overall lack of economic development in the Niger Delta within the context of the region's resource wealth relative to the welfare of the area's inhabitants as well as the contribution of oil extraction to the national economy at large. According to the writer, the crisis in the Niger Delta manifests as a model paradox of extreme poverty and underdevelopment within a region endowed with resource wealth, which has paved an increasingly significant role for civil society organisations and informal groups in filling the void created by a highly centralised and ineffective state. As a result, in arguing for an increased role for civil society organisations, the author argues for jurisdictional integrity in governance, which will necessitate the presence of units of government within specific spatial realms that, essentially, gives consent to citizens to pass judgment on the exercise of authority by government. This argument refers to the reassignment of responsibility and resources from the central government to a local unit, which necessitates the involvement of an array of non-state actors including civil society institutions, community organisations, and informal non-governmental associations. Within the context of local government, such institutions play a variety of complementary and parallel roles to the state institution while acting as a vehicle for enhancing the quality and variety of life in ways that are not in the arena of government. In this regard, this chapter put forward a position that explains that such groups can also act to compensate for the failures of centralised government systems, which are particularly endemic in Nigeria. Additionally, by conducting their activities in a co-operative manner, this chapter argues that civil society organisations can yield cohesiveness and better citizenship in a participatory democracy. Furthermore, it is of the view that civil society groups can provide protection not only from intrusive or neglectful government, but also from corporate power, by extending safeguards against discrimination and hazardous practices by private firms and multinational organisations. Among the active civil society groups in the region, the most widely recognised are the Movement for the Survival of the Ogoni People (MOSOP), the Supreme Egbesu Assembly (SEA), the Niger Delta Volunteer Force (NDVF), the Movement for the Emancipation of the Niger Delta (MEND), the Ijaw Youths Council (IYC), the Chikoko Movement (CM), the Movement for the Survival of the Ijaw Ethnic Nationality in the Niger Delta (MOSIEND),and the Movement for the Restoration of Ogbia (MORETO).

The preoccupation of the seventh chapter is the Niger Delta Technical Committee (NDTC), an organisation which was established in September 2008 to "collate, review and distil" the array of reports, suggestions and recommendations from previous accounts of the Niger Delta Crisis in order to institute alternative means of rectifying the long-standing dilemma in the region. By establishing a detailed analysis of the effectiveness of the NDTC, J. Shola Omotola's "Niger Delta Technical Committee (NDTC) and the Niger Delta Question" gauges the Committee's degree of success since its inception. Particularly, the author adopts a theoretical approach to evaluate the foundations of the NDTC with sufficient attention to the Com-

mittee's rationale, composition as well as its terms of the reference and reports. The key argument is that, from the historical context of the successive
failures of various bodies that have been tasked with addressing the long-
standing crisis in the Niger Delta, the NDTC is likely to be very limited
in its ability to successfully tackle the predicament. In addition, the writer
highlights the fundamental contradictions in policies of the NDTC. Furthermore, he asserts that the failure of the Committee can partly be attributed
to the lack of political will and insincerity on the part of the federal government with regard to the Niger Delta region. The author concludes that,
by and large, the formation of the NDTC served more as a source of hope
and expectation rather than a concrete means for the ultimate resolution of
the Niger Delta Crisis. Central to the contended failure of the Committee
are the inherent contradictions in the dynamics of the organisation, including the contention that no concrete steps have been taken towards achieving
the recommendations of the report on the Niger Delta as submitted by the
NDTC several months ago. Other factors which highlight the impending
failure of the NDTC are the creation of a separate Ministry of the Niger
Delta shortly after the establishment of the Committee and the line of rea-
soning that surmises that there is little indication that the present Yar'Adua
government will advance the efficiency of the Committee in light of the
electoral debacle. Finally, given the apparent limitations of the NDTC, the
author makes various recommendations on the potential of future measures
to address the crisis resolution effectively, and he further emphasises the
nature of the local and natural leadership as key structural challenges to
any potentially successful intervention.

Victor Ojakorotu and None Morake address the issue of the policies
adopted by Nigerian leaders towards the Niger Delta crisis in the eighth
chapter. According to the authors, the policies of the Nigerian state and the
oil multinationals have been largely inattentive to the plight of the inhabitants of the Niger Delta, who are subject to the undesirable consequences
of oil exploration. The analysis that this chapter offers is, therefore, situated in the nature of the political system as well as the policies adopted by
Nigerian leaders in the 1990s towards the crisis in the Niger Delta. This
lack of governmental accountability to the inhabitants of the Niger Delta
has been exacerbated by the extensive repression and authoritarianism of
successive governments. These scholars proffer analytical detail to the ex-

tent to which the repressive regimes worsened the unfolding Niger Delta Crisis through the ethnically based distribution of scarce resources. This style of leadership, coupled with the ethnic policies, has resulted in the polarisation of various groups in the country, and it resulted in the proliferation of ethnic, religious and communal conflicts during the 1980s and 1990s. The violence, also, exposes the virulent expression of long-standing frustration of the various groups, which inhabit the Niger Delta in response to the alienation and unfavourable policies of successive governments and oil multinationals. Violent action on the part of the region's inhabitants has been widely perceived as a means for attempting to transform the policies of the state and the foreign oil multinationals, although meaningful success has been limited. In relation to the policies of successive governments, the authors draw attention to the democratic rule under President Olusegun Obasanjo. Notwithstanding the high expectations with regard to policy shift and improved governance (especially towards the Niger Delta Crisis), the leadership of this government has also fallen short in effectively addressing the predicament. Conclusively, Ojakorotu and Morake assert that the abundance of oil in the Niger Delta, the distorted state and multinational policies that is accompanied by the diversity of an array of ethnic minorities significantly undermine the unity and governance of the troubled region. The authors point towards the necessity of Nigerian leaders to address the key concerns of the communities in the Niger Delta rather than pursuing repressive policies, which are detrimental to the region as well as the overall socio-economic and political environment in the country.

The ninth chapter, "The Democratisation of Violence in the Niger Delta of Nigeria: 1999-2007", addresses the issue of the prolonged violence in the Niger Delta. According to the author, J.M. Ayuba, the conflict is concentrated mainly in Bayelsa, Delta, Cross Rivers, Rivers, Ebonyi and Akwa Ibom. And his contribution traces the historical foundations of political violence in the Niger Delta by highlighting the disproportion between the increases in oil output and revenue on one hand, and the perpetual poverty and high levels of unemployment in the Niger Delta, as a central contributing factor on the other. The writer effectively provides historical substance to the proffered claims regarding the successive stages in the development of violence in the region, which affords a context to the violence that erupted in the region between 1999 and 2007. These phases, which the author bases on the work of Ogwuha Lemmy, are the development of violent struggles committed by armed gangs from the late 1990s to 2007: the peaceful protest and resistance of the 1970s and 1980. The harbinger of the second stage was effectively the use of brute force by the state as well as oil multinationals in suppressing protests, which led to the violence that persists to date. The third phase is represented by the reaction of local communities to Ken Saro-Wiwa and eight other Ogoni activists in 1995, an event which incited violent confrontations between the local communities in the Niger Delta and the oil companies and government. The final phase, which has continued from 1999 to the present day, is marked by a significant shift in the attitudes of militant groups and activists, who following the Kaiama Declaration in December 1998 express deep-seated concerns for resource control as opposed to development. The author's discussion, which concludes by highlighting the change in government's approach as evidenced by the Yar'Adua administration, points to a democratisation of the violence in the region, particularly signified by the recent amnesty deal of June 2009.

"Armed Militancy in the Niger Delta: The Subtlety of Amnesty Option and its Policy Implications for the Nigerian Political Economy" is this book's final chapter. Focusing on the amnesty granted to armed militias in the Niger Delta by the Nigerian government on June 22, 2009, Franklins A. Sanubi, analyses the ambivalence of such a policy towards combatants in contentious crisis. The author employs the theory of eufunctionism as a framework for analysing the context of the Niger Delta within the broader scope of political and economic developments in the region. To this extent, this chapter places the policy adopted towards the militias by the federal government within applicable schools of thought from eufunctionist theory, and it suggests that the good natured approach towards the militias reflects various subtleties that are best understood from a eufunctionist theory. The writer begins the development of his arguments by conceptualising the idea of amnesty, with a historical perspective regarding the definition as well as the granting of amnesty to other controversial figures in Nigeria's political history. Consequently, he reveals that the country has a long, well-documented history of extending amnesty to controversial political characters. The common trait in the examples this study gives is the attempt to pacify political friction, which largely results from the diversity of national groups that essentially embrace conflicting socio-political aspirations. This common characteristic of the amnesty cases situates the writer's analysis within the argument that the amnesty extended to the militias in the Niger Delta in June 2009 is contrary to accepted political economic conviction. To this extent, this chapter aims to analyse the implication of the amnesty declaration for the Niger Delta militants on the political economy of the Nigerian state, and it concludes that the policy adopted by the Nigerian government towards the militias in the Niger Delta could potentially provide a well-advised and beneficial policy for the resolution of the ongoing politico-economic conflict in the troubled region, which may serve as a remedy for future crises across the country.

# 2. The origins and the causes of crisis in the Niger Delta: The way forward

Dr. J.S. Oboreh

## Abstract

*The paper examines the origin and causes of the crisis in the Niger Delta. It x-rays the past effort of the federal government of Nigeria and oil companies to develop the area. The paper found that all past efforts lack seriousness and that they were mere political gimmicks aimed at continuous exploitation and marginalisation of the Niger Delta people. The paper posited that the failures of the political establishment to appreciate the fact that the continued neglect of the region by the government and the oil companies are a time bomb. The lingering crisis and the spate of abductions and killings are a response of the people of the Niger Delta for the deliberate marginalization of the region by the Nigerian government and the oil companies. The paper recommend among others; transparency and sincerity of purpose to put an end to the deceptive programmes and promises of successive governments and oil companies, creation of employment opportunities for the unemployed youths of the Niger Delta region, the need for a stake holders conference that will be free to discuss all matters relating to the region's development, and the need for a special project monitoring division to be established at the Presidency to monitor projects for which funds are being disbursed, in this way the Federal Government can be rest assured that the funds are used for infrastructural development and service to the citizens.*

## 2.1. Introduction

The Niger Delta, an area of approximately 26,000km$^2$ is the third largest delta area in the world. It is rich in the flora and fauna, and it accounts for about 90% of Nigeria's crude oil, which is the major plank upon which Nigeria's economy rests. Oil reserve at the region is put at about 25 billion barrels and gas reserve is put at about 130 trillion cubic feet. Aside from these reserves, the region is the second largest palm oil producer in the world next to Malaysia. It is, also, blessed with potentials in fishery, forest products, large clay deposits and good climatic conditions that support tourism and wild life (Abiye, 2005).

Prior to oil exploitation and exploration, the Niger Delta region had been a peaceful place with fishing and farming as the main means of livelihood of its denizens. Unfortunately, it had for long been ravaged by Europe's incursion, through slave trade as well as colonialism. However, since the advent of oil exploitation and exploration in the area, the Niger Delta region has suffered from environmental degradation and deprivation. And, as a result, the traditional means of livelihood for the people of that region have been destroyed and truncated. This prevailing deprivation and neglect have provoked the current crises in the region; this situation is not only tearing the area apart, but it is, also, ravaging the whole country (Akaruese, 1998).

Since pre-colonial days, the Niger Delta region has played a crucial role in the Nigerian economy. Its ports and rivers provided access for the British to penetrate the Nigerian hinterland; these facilities were the gateway for the trade in slaves, and they later served as the exit points for the exported commodities from the South of Nigeria such as palm produce, timber and rubber, and groundnut and cotton from the distant northern parts of the country. However, the region has not benefitted directly from the many economic activities because the environmental conservation and the economic development of the Niger Delta area depend on the in-flow of federal funding and goodwill into the region. The extent of such benevolence is dependent on improved relations between the national government and the people of the Niger Delta. The frosty relationship in existence between the state and the people of the Niger Delta, on one hand, and between the multinational oil companies and the people of the region, on the other hand, has not allowed any significant development to take place in the region. In spite of this, the people of the region, over time, employed different methods, strategies and means, in the past, to draw attention of the political establishment to their plight, and to the fact that the continued neglect of the region by the government and the oil companies was a time bomb. These peaceful actions were of no effect. Today, the lingering crisis and the spate of abductions and killings in the region are the responses of the people of the Niger Delta to the deliberate marginalisation of the region by the Nigerian government and the oil companies.

## 2.2. Niger Delta territorial space: reason for poor compensation programme

The territorial space of the Niger Delta region has been defined with political coloration. According to official definition by the state, the Niger Delta region is synonymous with the Oil Producing States in Nigeria. In this context, therefore, the Niger Delta comprises nine (9) Nigerian states namely: Abia, Imo, Edo, Delta, Rivers, Bayelsa, Cross River, Akwa-Ibom and Ondo States. This definition is what informs the Niger Delta Development Commission (NDDC) Bill (Yomere, 2007). Thus, the Niger Delta Development Commission interprets the Niger Delta region as the Oil Producing States of Nigeria. Part I Subsection 2(1), which deal with the establishment of NDDC, and the ethnic groups (States) who shall be members of the Commission, clearly shows what the Niger Delta Act intends to solve is the problem of the Oil Producing States and not necessarily that of the Niger Delta region *per se*. There can never be any meaningful development programme or compensation for oil exploitation in the Niger Delta region within this framework, especially with the governors of various states in Nigeria jostling for the inclusion of their states as constituent parts of the Niger Delta. In essence, if the long years of crude oil exploration in Sokoto and the Chad basin in northern Nigeria have yielded positive results, they too would have been included as member states of the Niger Delta Development Commission (Ifowodo and Edos, 2008).

The fact is this: there is a major difference between Oil Producing States and the Niger Delta States. The need for this distinction is as a result of the peculiar terrain of the Niger Delta region and the problems associated with the area. These are not shared qualities with every state that is listed as an Oil Producing State in Nigeria. Therefore, the Niger Delta region and the Oil Producing States must neither be confused nor used interchangeably. It is important to acknowledge that the Niger Delta has to be meaningfully and comprehensively defined taking into cognisance its unique characteristics in order for the Nigerian government to come up with meaningful programmes that will be useful to the people of the region, and that will serve their communal interest. The people of the Niger Delta region are the ones who are exposed to oil pollution and environmental degradation, and who have suffered from neglect and poor infrastructural development (Aiyetan, 2008).

Geographically, the Niger Delta region is the area within the lower Niger River at Onya that divides into an eastward running Nun River and a westward running Forcados River. Both rivers break into series of tributaries, creeks, streams and rivulets, which join the tributaries of twenty-two (22) costal rivers in the complicated network of water channels separated by soggy, muddy land mass. The area has one of the largest wetlands of the world with swamps crisscrossing rivers, rivulets, creeks tributaries and distributaries of the majestic River Niger, and it comprises freshwater swamp forest, alone covering about half of the delta, lowland equatorial monsoon, brackish water and sand barriers. Thus, the Niger Delta region is contained within a triangular outline with apex town of Aboh being the northern top most. The Benin River fringes from the west boundary of the ecological region of the Nigerian lowland forest region. The Imo River marks the eastern extent where it merges into Cross-Niger transition forest. Finally, the southern side of the Niger Delta swamp forest is separated from the Atlantic by a band of mangrove of total area of about $15,000$ km$^2$ to make it the third largest delta in the world. Thus, it is located between latitude $5^0$ 15' N and $6^0$ 00' N of the equator and between longitude $5^0$ $4^1$ E and $6^0$ 25' E (Fregene, 2000).

Generally found in this thick evergreen forest are diverse animals and plant species with flora and fauna dominated by massive mangroves belt, water hyacinth, patches of rainforest and variegated land for the inhabitants. This is the difficult terrain with the thick evergreen forest known as the Delta of the Niger or simply the Niger Delta. This is the region that was highlighted in the Berlin Conference on Environment and Development in 1978 with is peculiar terrain and peculiar development needs that deserved special attention and the understanding of all (Block, 2004).

Linguistically, ethnographically and culturally, the Niger Delta of the pre-crude oil and gas era comprised a bewildering mix of ethnic groups: the Ijaw, the Itsekiri, Urhobo, Isoko, Ikwerre, part of Kwale and Akwa Ibom. The issue of population distribution in density, and the pattern of settlement in the Niger Delta are largely determined by the availability of dry land as well as the nature of the physical landscape of the region. The Niger Delta region has a low relief and poor ground drainage. The factor is responsible for the paucity of settlements of considerable size in the heartland of the Niger Delta. Large settlements are found in the interior parts of the Delta where drainage conditions and accessibility are better (Eson, 2000).

The mangrove swamp zone interspersed by islands of dray land, such as Port Harcourt, Sapele, Ughelli, Warri, etc., present habitable settlement located at the head of the navigable limits of the coastal rivers or estuaries. On the other hand, settlements at the sea front such as Burutu, Forcados, Ogidigben, Gborodo, Madangho, Oporoza, Ozoro, Uzere, Otujeremi Bille, etc are made particularly difficult by their poor accessibility to the major population centres in the hinterland. In addition, most brackish water eco-zones are very hostile to live in (Ezeobi, 2008).

In the absence of reliable statistical data, it suffices to say that, since the 1991 population census, there are indications that the population of the Niger Delta states have been on the increase. The regular influx to the oil-producing states by people in search of employment opportunities has greatly increased, and there is also high population density on habitable land in the riverrine and coastal areas due to oil drilling (Freire, 2002).

The major human occupations in the Niger Delta region may be categorised under three main headings: primary, secondary and tertiary occupations. The major traditional primary occupation includes farming and fishing, while the secondary occupations include industries like gin distillation, textiles weaving, boat carving, etc. Tertiary occupation includes trade and commerce, transportation etc.

## 2.3. Infrastructural deficiencies in the Niger Delta

Infrastructure is usually defined as the underlying basic building, institutions and facilities or other essential elements that are necessary to enable and sustain growth and development of a community. Larimer (1994) speaks of this as the underlying foundation or framework of basic services upon which the growth and development of an area, community or a system depend. Infrastructure, therefore, includes a broad spectrum of services, institutions and facilities that range from transportation systems and public utilities to finance systems, laws and law enforcement agencies, and educational facilities. This definition brings clearly to light the significance of infrastructural development in any society since its absence hampers the economy of such an area. This lack of infrastructure is the bane of the Niger Delta, and four reasons can be adduced for the deficiencies of infrastructural development in the Niger Delta region. These are:

## a. Difficult terrain

To allay the fears of the minority indigenes of the Niger Delta and to address the developmental needs of the peculiar terrain of the region, the British government set up the Willinks Commission in 1957. The Commission's 1958 Report recommended that the Niger Delta deserved special developmental attention, and that the region should be declared a "Special Federal Territory". The special area implied by the Report covered all the present Bayelsa and Rivers Sates and parts of the present Delta State from the mouth of Forcardos River to Andoni River. In fact, one of their proposals was the development of a canal from Port Harcourt to Warri, which should reduce water travel times considerably.

The lack of seriousness on the part of the Federal Government of Nigeria to address the needs of the Niger Delta people is exemplified by the fact that the Niger Delta Development Board (NDDB), which was established to handle the development challenges of the Niger Delta, fizzled into oblivion in 1960 with little or nothing to show for its years of existence. Not even the canal project was ever started (Novak, 2000).

The Niger Delta Special Area and its board were replaced by the Niger Delta Basin Development Authority (NDBDA) in 1978. It was given similar spatial jurisdiction and features as the NDDB. The dissolution of the Special Area and its board became an imperative due to the creation of ten (10) other River Basin Authorities designed to cater for other parts of Nigeria. With this new arrangement, the eleven (11) River Basin Authorities were categories under different priority criteria. This made it possible for some of the River Basin Authorities to demand least attention. In this way, the marginalisation plan for the Niger Delta region was concretised (Shaaba, 1998). Thus, acclaimed efforts by the federal government at developing the Niger Delta region are in actual sense political gimmicks because political consideration rather than equity, fair play and justice or, more importantly, natural geographical features determined the demarcation of the country into River Basin Authorities: the whole of Niger Delta region had the head office of only one (1) of the eleven (11) River Basin Authorities. In a country like Nigeria where the coastal zone is bathed in Atlantic waters from 25 major estuaries and many other major tributaries of rivers in a network of waterways, it was the height of marginalisation bothering on criminal neglect to create only the Niger Delta Basin Development Authority to cater for all major rivers of Rivers in Bayelsa and Delta States (Oyebode, 2000).

### b. The Oil Mineral Producing Areas Development Commission (OMPADEC)

The mounting agitation for the development of the Niger Delta region since so much petrol-dollar is generated from the region led to the establishment of the Oil Mineral Producing Area Development Commission (OMPADEC). It was set up to bring about a speedy development of the Niger Delta region and the people of the oil producing communities.

Members of the management staff were carefully selected by the Head of State with the connivance of the military state governors in order to ensure that contracts and monies were released based on directives from Aso Rock, which is Nigeria's seat of government. However, the majority of the contractors who had the plumiest jobs came from outside OMPADEC states (Yomere, 2007).

As a result, it was quite clear from the onset that OMPADEC was not set up to develop the Niger Delta areas: it was a channel through which the petrol-dollar could be siphoned away for the benefits of friends and loyalists of people in government. This finds expression in the fact that OMPADEC never had a vision and, thus, there was no master plan to guide the operation of the Commission. In addition, a good number of the successful contractors never reported to site once they got their mobilisation fees, and no measures were ever taking by the Commission to recover such monies. Even those who moved to site later abandoned their projects (Ofeimun, (2008). The present Niger Delta Development Commission (NDDC) as set up is on a better pedestal than OMPADEC. The Commission has produced a master plan for the development of the oil producing areas inclusive of the Niger Delta region.

It is hoped that in the face of increasing restiveness and violence in the Niger Delta, which are arising from poor compensation practices by the oil companies and the federal government, the government shall grant the Commission the freehand to adhere strictly to the master plan.

### c. Political allegiance to Abuja

The process for nomination and qualification of candidates for all elections are clearly outlined in the national constitution and, also, in the constitutions of the various political parties. However, the political establishment in Abuja believes that it has the inalienable right to the oil wealth of the Niger Delta region. Against this background, the federal government is highly interested and, indeed, it decides on who contests for which position in the region. In other words, the people of the area are denied the opportunity to nominate who should contest for what position. Consequently, the elected officials from the region own their allegiance to those in Abuja. As a result, they are largely unresponsive to the needs and aspirations of their people because they tend to believe that as long as they pay homage to their sponsors at Abuja, they would enjoy the protection of their godfathers rather than the people of their local councils or constituencies. This strange dynamics fuel the elected officials' constant need to stash enough monies to meet the demands of their political career as orchestrated by their political godfathers. To achieve the goal of embezzlement, fathom projects are cooked up and false reports that seemingly justify the squandered billions of naira are generated. The end result is the lack of infrastructural development in the region (Yomere 2007).

In many of the states of the Niger Delta region, the eight years of civilian administration have only brought dissatisfaction to the people of the area: the people live in abject poverty; there is palpable neglect; the roads are very bad; there is the lack of portable drinking water; the general hospitals are devoid of drugs; the school buildings are dilapidated; the people of the Niger Delta are frustrated.

### d. Corruption and culture of impunity

In his address to the nation on Democracy Day (2005), President Olusegun Obasanjo said that "corruption kills innovation, creativity, compromises public morality, contaminates the individuals and collective dignity, distorts national plans and erodes dignity and commitment to hard work and the dignity of labour" (Yomere, 2007). Sadly, corruption has become institutionalised in the Nigerian society: it has become a norm; it is a part and parcel of the Nigerian culture and, subsequently, it has gone into the realm of the behaviour of the Nigerian people. Accordingly, value system in the Nigerian nation has changed; good name, honestly, integrity have now given way to little work and the inordinate desire for the acquisition of wealth at the expense of public good (Yomere, 2007). Against this background, there can only be good democratic governance if the administration develops institutions and processes which control human craving for power, greed and inclination to graft and corruption (Taiwo, 2000).

It is the desire to carry anti-graft war that gave birth to such institutions and mechanisms like the Economic and Financial Crime Commission (EFCC) and the Independent Corrupt Practices and other Related Offences Commission (ICPC). Reports abound in the electronic and print media about Nigerian politicians who are secretly buying houses that cost millions of pounds and dollars abroad. They steal the people's money and stash it away in foreign accounts. Political leaders in the Niger Delta are no exception (Yomere, 2007).

Nigerians are overwhelmed with the ongoing trial of some ex-governors, who are accused of stealing public monies in accounts overseas. These are public monies that should have been used for the provision of social services and infrastructure for the general good.

## 2.4. Oil companies and the Niger Delta

Oil companies continue to make huge profits, and the Nigerian state continues to amass wealth whereas the Niger Delta undergoes continues exploitation, underdevelopment, and neglect. Expressing this situation more succinctly, Olorode (1998) observes that "over 90% of Nigeria's exported earning accrues from sale of crude oil and form the bedrock of private accusation by various ethnic wings of Nigeria's ruling class, yet most of the roads in the Niger Delta region (where they exist) are in despicable shape." While oil made a positive impact on the Nigerian state, oil operation made a negative indelible mark on the Niger Delta region and its people. While oil brought Nigeria to limelight at international level through unprecedented wealth, the same oil has brought pains and sorrow to the Niger Delta people (Toyo, 2000).

In the main, the operations of the oil industry and the behaviour of the various Nigerian governments have produced two major negative effects. First, there is the environmental pollution which encompasses the terrestrial, atmospheric and marine environments. The second is that the proceeds from the exploited oil are used to service other parts of the country to the neglect of the oil producing area. The revenue allocation formula, particularly since the 1979, fails to take into consideration the high cost of providing basic socio-economic infrastructure because of the swampy terrain of the area (Olorode, 1998). The second aspect is that the revenue sharing formula has been in favour of those geo-political units with relatively high population even though population figure in Nigeria remain controversial. Thus, Olorode (1998) noted that in spite of the fact that the sub-region has accounted for more that 70% of government revenue and 90% of foreign exchange earnings, it is the one suffering from obvious under development problems.

## 2.5. The environment and the oil Industry

Oil exploitation started in the Niger Delta region a long time ago before attention was paid to the environmental concerns of the area. Thus, Soremekun and Obadare (1998) observed that, although the shipment of oil from the Nigerian coast in commercial quantifies started as far back as 1958, it was not until some thirty (30) years later that attention was drawn to the havoc being wreaked on the environment by the oil companies. As pointed out by Soremekun and Obadare (1998), petroleum operations in the Niger Delta have engendered massive environmental pollution in the oil producing areas of the region. Specifically, there have been pipeline leakages as well as blow-outs and spillages which have had severe effects on land, water resources, the micro-climate and the economic activities of the residents. The unquantifiable consequences of these have been environmental degradation, health hazard, loss of valuable agricultural land and settlements. This led Amadi and Tamuo (2001) to conclude that oil exploitation activities in the Niger Delta has impacted adversely on the life of the people. As more oil is exploited and taken away, more devastation is left behind, and the petro-dollar earned does not benefit the people where lives have been shattered by oil.

The effects of the operations of the oil companies on the environment are not only devastating, but they have triggered off series of crises. As rightly noted by Oloruntimehin and Ayoade (2002), most of the conflicts have arisen from complex environmental problems and a long history of basic neglect and the lack of social development of the peoples who have watched helplessly as their land and water resources are continually visited by devastation through intensive exploitation and exploration of petroleum and gases.

## 2.6. Economic, political and social consequences of the oil Industry in the Niger Delta

The social-economic and political implications of the activities of the oil companies in the Niger Delta region have to do with exploitation, marginalisation, underdevelopment, impoverishment and the attendant crises in the region. This situation has remained for so long in spite of the various pronouncements of the successive governments and their so-called palliative measures. However, it is pertinent to emphasise that the course and direction of activities and operations of the oil companies and the Nigerian state in the Niger Delta area are basically political issues. And, like Ihonvbere (2000) rightly observes, Nigerian politics is full of painful paradoxes. On the one hand, the country's politics carries the stamp of confused, fractionalised, and extremely corrupt elite with a limited sense of nationhood. The failure of the state to take appropriate decisions or actions that would ameliorate the suffering of the people of the Niger Delta region attests to the nature and motive of the state and the elite, who are responsible for such decision. Hence, Ihonvbere (2000) argues that the character of the Nigerian state continues to be directly responsible for reproducing the country's deepening socio-economic and political contradictions. In fact, the state seems to worsen the country's predicaments with every policy action or inaction it initiates or fails to initiate in the process of trying to consolidate the interest of its custodians.

## 2.7. The way forward

The answer to the question of the future of the Niger Delta region hinges on three major assumptions: one, if the current strategy of hide and seek adopted by the federal government continues, the area would continue to experience unprecedented turbulence and insecurity; two, failure to have radical shift in government policy and action that would engender social and favourable distribution of revenue among the constituents in the country would only prolong the crises in the area; three, the more the ethnic militias in the Niger Delta benefit financially from the on-going hostage taking, the more they would sustain it and the more difficult the oil companies will find it difficult to operate.

President Musa Umar Yar'Adua's government started on a good footing, having in place the NDDC Master Plan – a project that takes a holistic approach to the problems of the region. The NDDC Master plan has the potentials to right the wrongs of the past if properly funded and implemented. The Master plan is, thus, the pivot around which this study's discussion on the way forward shall revolve.

## a. Transparency and sincerity of purpose

The endless and deceptive programmes and promises of successive governments (both military and civilian) and oil companies, which the people of the Niger Delta have been fed, have given rise to a deep-rooted distrust and cynicism toward anything that the federal government or the oil companies will do to alleviate the problems of the Niger Delta people. Against this background, the President must demonstrate in words and in deed a high level of sincerity. He must be sincere and transparent in every action taken in connection with the region (Yomere, 2007). He must minimise or reduce to the barest minimum every form of manipulative strategies, de-emphasise the use of military force for solving political problems, and rely more on communication and dialogue with all stakeholders in the region. Political problems should receive political solution instead of the use of brutal military force. The President should be seen to give all stakeholders equal treatment, in his handling of the Niger Delta issues otherwise the already existing suspicion will be magnified (Yomere, 2007).

### b. Stakeholders' Conference

The various ground works at the presidency in preparation for convey-ing a conference of all stake holders in the region is highly welcomed. If the conference is to usher in peace and stability in the Niger Delta re-gion, the people should be given the free hand to choose who should repre-sent them. The federal government should discourage either herself and the many state governments from imposing the so-called public figures, polit-ical or community leaders on the people. Any leader who is worth its salt should present himself or herself to the people at the ward level through the council level for selection through a transparent electoral process. The con-ference should be open to discuss any issue of interest. There should not be "a no-go area". The vexed issue of resource control should be exhaustively discussed and a derivation formula that is acceptable to all parties arrived at. It is very important that an acceptable solution should be reached since other mineral resources in the country are not nationalised like petroleum and gas. It is only fair that all mineral resources be subjected to the same law. It is unfair that those whose land contain gold, tin, bauxite, etc can explore them freely while those whose lands contain petroleum are totally deprived. Whatever decision is arrived at in respect of the derivation for-mula can also apply across board to all other mineral resources. In this way, the people of the Niger Delta region will no longer have the feeling of being exploited. The implementation can be in phases over a five year period in order to avoid budgetary shock to the non-oil producing states. Besides, this is likely to encourage the exploration and production of other mineral resources throughout Nigeria.

## c. Employment generation

The level of unemployment in the Niger Delta area is very alarming and disturbing, particularly among the youths. To address this issue, there is the urgent need for job creation. Oil companies must employ their staff from the Niger Delta region. A situation where more than 97% of senior and management staff of oil companies are from outside the region can no longer be acceptable (Yomere, 2008). The provision of jobs hinges on the existence of, at least, basic infrastructure that will enable entrepreneurs to exploit the economic opportunities available. However, it must be observed that considering the exploited, deprived, and impoverished nature of the Niger Delta people, the provision of infrastructure within the context of the NDDC Master Plan requires the concerted efforts of NDDC, the federal and states governments and the organised private sector.

The following aspects require urgent attention:

1. **Health**

Health is wealth. A healthy nation, therefore, is a wealthy nation. Over the years, the health sector, especially in the riverrine areas, had been neglected. The so-called cottage hospitals in the riverrine areas are understaffed; drugs and equipment are chronically scarce. The health sector must receive a lot of focus because of its key role in the development of the region. Funding of the health care system should not be left alone for the NDDC and state governments; rather the federal government should play an active role in resuscitating the existing ones and building new ones.

To address the issue of understaffing of hospitals, special reverine allowance should be introduced and high enough to attract medical personnel to the rural and riverrine areas.

2. **Manufacturing**

Some level of industrial development is required in the Niger Delta region, which will make possible the creation of jobs to the teeming population of the Niger Delta region, especially the youths. To attain this goal, there is the urgent need to provide some level of infrastructure such as a good road network connecting the riverrine areas with the hinterland, transportation (land and water), electricity that can be generated from the abundant gas in the region, water (for drinking and industrial use), education, housing, skill acquisition centres and the development of human resources.

Creating the enabling environment that will facilitate the growth of industry in the Niger Delta region is the responsibility of the federal, state governments and the NDDC. Specifically, the many layers of government should identify a number of strategic sectors, tackle the bottleneck associated with them; and, then, allow entrepreneurs to drive growth in these sectors and create jobs. Where state and local government development capacity is lacking, the state should partner with reputable development professionals who have demonstrated commitment to community participation in planning and implementation. The development concept has to expand beyond satisfying the parochial oil – communities / local council and be positioned within a regional socio-economic development matrix, in which efforts is made to offer opportunities and attraction to all people of the Niger Delta.

3. **Agriculture**

Efforts should be made to realise the agricultural potentials of the area. Government needs to put in place viable policies backed by proper funding, implementation and monitoring. The starting point of the agricultural development programme should be the peasant farmers. They must be encouraged to do this until agriculture has become mechanised and there are sufficient industrial activities to transform the peasantry to industrial producers.

Farm input, chemicals, equipment and machinery should be subsidised for farmers. The federal government should strengthen agriculture research institutes whose research findings can be applied to peasant farming by proper extension service. To improve the coverage of these extension services, the peasant farmers should be grouped together into Farmers Cooperative Societies.

4. **Access to Finance**

Access to finance remains a major log jam for small business development in Nigeria, particularly in the Niger Delta area. The central problem here is that both domestic saving rates and domestic private credit are very low in Nigeria. Nigeria, therefore, need to examine micro finance initiatives seriously; if the country were to stimulate some village-level economic development, then micro finance can be empowering by assisting poor people, especially women, with small loans that will enable them invest in various productive activities.

5. **Fight against corruption**

The fight against corruption must be intensified by strengthening the institutions and mechanisms put in place to fight this monster. Drastic reduction in the level of corruption will significantly uplift the standard of living of the citizenry. Governments and NDDC funds that are wasted through questionable sources should be stopped. Resources that are channelled to foreign accounts in Europe and America through over-invoicing and bribery should be made available for investment in social services. Against this background, the Nigerian president should put his weight and unwavering support behind EFCC and ICPC irrespective of whose ox is gored.

6. **Special project monitoring division**

There is the need for a special project monitoring division to be established in the presidency. In this way, the federal government can ensure transparency and accountability in the use of the funds disbursed to states in the Niger Delta region. Through the monitoring of the projects for which funds are being disbursed, the state can be rest assured that the funds are used for infrastructural development and service to the citizens.

And as a strategy for enduring peace; there is the need for the G-8 countries, European Union and the United Nations to pressurise all governments that host oil companies operations in the Niger Delta area to adhere to human rights principles, and see as a matter of obligation the development of the area and the attainment of good life by the people of the area. The international community also has a role to play in trying to broker peace and welfare enforcement in the area. Sincerity on the part of the international community would give the agitators and militants in the area some confidence that the dawn of a new hope has come. The international community must clearly provide for sanctions against defaulters to the peace and welfare enforcement resolution.

## 2.8. Conclusion

Previous governments had neglected the people of the Niger Delta region. The people suffered hardship, deprivation and underdevelopment. All entreaties from the people of the region for the federal government to provide social amenities and economic development of the area fell on deaf ears. Rather, arrogance, politics of deceit, the belief in the efficacy of the principle of "divide and rule" and, especially, the belief that internal problems demanding political solutions can better be settled by brutal military force blinded the federal government to the fact that a time bomb is waiting to explode in the Niger Delta. The ingredient that facilitated the explosion came when the youths of the Niger Delta participated in the "Abacha One Million Man March" in Abuja. It then dawned on them where and how the wealth from the Niger Delta is used. It is this revelation that triggered what is today known as the Niger Delta crisis.

The federal government is now showing some signs of seriousness. The democratic government under President Olusegun Obasanjo set up the NDDC to address these grievances. The NDDC has been empowered to provide the needed infrastructure befitting an area which has contributed so much to the national purse. "Better late than never" so the saying goes. The Niger Delta region has come to appreciate the need for equity, fair play and justice, which are the foundation of peaceful coexistence.

## 2.9. References

Abiye, S.O. (2005) "A Review of Some Conceptual Issues on Resource Control in Nigeria" in Orobator, E.

Ifowodo, F., & Edos, E. (eds.) Federal State and Resource Control in Nigeria. Benin City: F. Parker publishing Company

Aiyetan, D. (2008) "Oil Has Been a Blessing a Curse" in Tell, February, 18

Akaruese, L. (1998) "Crisis in Oil Yielding Communities: Causes and Dimensions" in Olorode, O. Raji, W., Ogunye, J. & Oladunjoye, T. (eds.) Ken Saro Wiwa and the Crises of the Nigerian State. Lagos: Committee for the Defence of Human Rights (cdhr)

Atsegbua, L. Akpotaire, V. & Dimowo, F. (2004) Environmental Law in Nigeria: Theory and Practice, Lagos: Ababa Press Limited.

Block, W. (2004) Social Justice. LewRockwell.com

Eson, P.O. (2000) "The Political Economy of Oil Extraction in Nigeria" in Raji, W., Ale, A., & Akinsola E. (eds.) A cdhr Publication on the Crisis in the Oil Producing Communities in Nigeria. Lagos: Committee for the Defence of Human Rights (cdhr).

Ezeobi, (2008) "50 Depressing years of Oil in Nigeria" in Punch, February 17

Fregene, P. (2000) "How Nigeria Plundered and Underdeveloped Itsekiri People" in Raji, W., Ale, A., & Akinsola E. (eds.) A cdhr Publication on the Crisis in the Oil Producing Communities in Nigeria. Lagos: Committee for the Defence of Human Rights (cdhr).

Freire, P. (1970) Pedagogy of the Oppressed. Continuum Publishing Company

Gindin, S. (2002) Anti-Capitalism and the Terrain of Social Justice. Monthly Review, vol. 53, No. 9

Ihonvbere, J. (2000) "A Recipe for Perpetual Crises: The Nigerian State and the Niger Delta Question" in Raji, W., Ale, A., & Akinsola E. (eds.) A cdhr Publication on the Crisis in the Oil Producing Communities in Nigeria. Lagos: Committee for the Defence of Human Rights (cdhr).

Novak, M. (2000) Defining Social Justice. First Things: A Journal of Religion, Culture and Public life.

Ofeimun, O. (2000) "The Legal Framework of Oil Extraction in Nigeria" in Raji, W., Ale, A., & Akinsola E. (eds.) A cdhr Publication on the Crisis in the Oil Producing Communities in Nigeria. Lagos: Committee for the Defence of Human Rights (cdhr).

Olorode, O. (1998) "Imperialism, Neocolonialism and the Extractive Industries in Nigeria" in Olorode, O. Raji, W., Ogunye, J. & Oladunjoye, T. (eds.) Ken Saro Wiwa and the Crises of the Nigerian State. Lagos: Committee for the Defence of Human Rights (cdhr)

Oloruntimehin, B.O. and Ayoade, J. A.A. (2002) "An Overview of Conflicts in Nigeria: 1984-2000" Ibadan: Development Policy Centre.

Omoweh, D. (2000) "Oil Exploration in Nigeria – A Theoretical Overview" in Raji, W., Ale, A., & Akinsola E. (eds.) A cdhr Publication on the Crisis in the Oil Producing Communities in Nigeria. Lagos: Committee for the Defence of Human Rights (cdhr).

Oyebode, A. (2000) "The Legal Framework of Oil Exploration in Nigeria – A critique" in Raji W. Ale and Akinsola E. (eds) Boiling Point Lagos: CDHR Publication

Oyeshola, D.O.P. (1998) Politics of International Environmental Regulations. Ibadan: Daily Graphics (Nigeria) Limited.

Rawals, J. (1971) A Theory of Justice. Oxford: Oxford University Press

Sha'aba, A. (1998) "MOSOP and the Ogoni Struggle" in Olorode, O. Raji, W.,

Ogunye, J. & Oladunjoye, T. (eds.) Ken Saro Wiwa and the Crises of the Nigerian State. Lagos: Committee for the Defence of Human Rights (cdhr)

Soremekun, K. Obadare, E. (1998) "The Politics of Oil Corporations in Nigeria" in Olorode, O. Raji, W., Ogunye, J. & Oladunjoye, T. (eds.) Ken Saro Wiwa and the Crises of the Nigerian State. Lagos: Committee for the Defence of Human Rights (cdhr)

Taiwo, F. (2000) "Nigeria and other Oil Producing Countries – A Comparative Analysis of Oil Revenue Sharing Formula" in Raji, W. Ale, A., A., & Akinsola E. (eds.) A cdhr Publication on the Crisis in the Oil Producing Communities in Nigeria. Lagos Committee for the Defence of Human Rights (cdhr)

Toyo, E. (2000) "Chairman's Opening Comments" in Raji, W. Ale, A., A., & Akinsola E. (eds.) A cdhr Publication on the Crisis in the Oil Producing Communities in Nigeria. Lagos Committee for the Defence of Human Rights (cdhr)

Yomere, G. O. (2007). "The dearth of Infrastructural Development in the Niger Delta and the Way Forward". A paper Presented at the Inauguration of the Nigerian Institute of Quantity Surveyors Asaba, Delta State. Sept. 29, 2007.

# 3. Oil and democracy in Nigeria: oiling the friction?

Henry Alapiki and Fidelis Allen [1]

## Abstract

*Oil in Nigeria has become to the polity what the blood is to the natural body. Paradoxically, the oil seems to have at the same time constituted a source of friction that threatens democracy and development in Nigeria. Why is it so? We argue that the mode of extraction and distribution of the oil revenue is mutually antagonistic to democracy. Since extraction of the oil must continue, and since the state will continue to depend on it for the running of its affairs for a long time, political leaders inescapably undermine democratic values. An important signpost of this argument is seen in the manner in which political leaders struggle for political power. They fear losing elections by competitive liberal democratic processes void of malpractice but do all that they can to remove all uncertainties in such elections. The question is this: is oil oiling the friction? Apparently, the struggle is both to maintain the extraction of oil and distribution of the oil revenue that funds the state. The consequences include loss of property rights by some fragments of the society and attainment of development which defines the essence of democracy.*

## 3.1. Introduction

There is no one oil producing country in Africa without acute problems of political and economic development, and of violent conflicts among groups and the state. In short, predictions of proliferation of wars about natural resources seem to be coming true with many of these countries. Since oil became a strategic commodity, both for the state in Nigeria and her overseas partners, politics, society and the economy have been characterised by conflict, many times, violent relationships among key actors in the system. Two major phases of this scenario can be identified in the case of Nigeria: first, oil in the context of military regimes, and, then, oil and democracy. The nature of politics of oil during military regimes and that of a democracy should differ markedly, since democracies, normatively, are said to

---

[1]  Being a paper presented at the annual conference of the Nigerian Political Science Association, NPSA held at the University of Port Harcourt-27th-29th August, 2006

possess high conflict resolution potentials because of their people-oriented policies and ability of citizens to limit the powers of the state. However, the reverse is the case for Nigeria because democracy is yet to resolve the friction emerging from extraction of oil, distribution of revenue accruing from it and the dependence of the state on it. Besides, the state appears disrespectful of groups' rights and she is determined not to have its powers limited by the people on issues pertaining to the extraction of oil and distribution of its revenue. This essay sets out to explain why oil is and will continue to be a source of hostility in Nigeria, and how its mode of extraction, distribution of revenue and dependence of the state on it for revenue work contrary to developmental democratic ideals.

The paper relied mainly on secondary data, and it argues that the oil related conflict in Nigeria's Niger Delta region is a typology of resource war. And, it is the position of this study that democracy has had no effect on fixing the war for two obvious reasons: an economy has emerged out of the resource war; democracy is not developmental in Nigeria.

## 3.2. Key Variables

Researches on democracy have always focused on either socio-economic or politico-institutional traditions, and rarely do they train their lenses on both at the same time. Therefore, the exception found in the work of Diskin Abraham, Diskin Hanna and Hazan Reuven (2005) is appealing. It establishes the framework for analysing the mutual impact of the key variables of oil, democracy, development and friction, which have been well reflected in literature. Although at the level of practical politics in Nigeria the variables have turned into mere rhetoric, academic discourse on democracy continues to include these variables in explaining the Nigerian condition.

The key institutional variable is federalism, which has to do with a type of regime with concentration of power at the centre. It fuels the assumption that autonomy in the generation and control of resources by the co-ordinate units of government will generate less violent conflicts among groups and between them and the state in federations. The other variable is a societal variable of ethnic minority marginalisation.The hypothesis deriving from this variable is based on what is available in literature that suggests that ethnic grievances against the state on economic marginalisation and unresponsiveness of democracy to such grievances create strains for democracy.

Federalism as an institutional political arrangement is widely researched, and Nigeria is often mentioned as a federation. However, normative definitions and the principles of federalism have contradicted the functioning of federal institutions thereby leading to the need for either a reconceptualisation of the idea of federalism or the perpetuation of a condition of high pessimism about the federal status of Nigeria. A critique of federalism as practiced in Nigeria is a serious political issue for Nigerians. Unfortunately, its discourse appears to have been the preoccupation of politicians for which the structure and the character of the state has also been implicated for its nature of distribution of power and resources. This is more so since oil became a strategic commodity.

A careful perusal of the concept of federalism in Nigeria suggests that it has been shaped more by ethnicities rather than by any objective need. But, this has historical root in the colonial-contrived idea of Hausa-Fulani hegemony as a consequence of the amalgamation in 1914 (Momoh, 2003:164). Initially, contestation over federalism took the form of a struggle to access and control power. Later the struggle became inspired by the need to access revenue from oil extraction. Apparently, the South, having been denied of development and power, resorted to articulating its grievances on the basis of the oil wealth and its distribution in Nigeria. There is no suggestion here that the south-south is united in this struggle.

The restructuring of the country has, therefore, been a seeming hegemonising response of the Hausa-Fulani, Ibos and Yoruba, to both the struggle for power and control of resources by aggrieved minority regions endowed with the oil resources. This present structure of federalism reinforces, nonetheless, the hegemonic grand plan of indigenous colonialists, which then explains the seeming unconstitutional challenge of the system by oil producing communities. Because the state in Nigeria is dominated by the trinity of Hausa-Fulani, Ibo and Yoruba, it is easy to comprehend the nature of the conspiracy against the minority people of the Niger Delta, and swiftly indict the state for its negative role in the undemocratic and slow economic development of oil producing regions of Nigeria. This speaks volume on the character of the state as an obstacle to federal democracy in Nigeria (Ihonvbere, 2003: 187).

To better understand the dynamics of federalism in Nigeria in relation
to the friction between the state and the social forces in the Niger Delta
region, it is important to x-tray the political economy of oil extraction in
Nigeria, the distribution of national revenue, and the character of the state.
According to Ihonvbere:

... the state, privatised by the corrupt elite to substitute for its tenuous relation to
productive activities, relies on violence, repression, and other forms of manipula-
tion to reproduce itself and maintain a form of domination.

Thus, federalism is far more than a mere political arrangement. Its functioning has large-scale implications for economic and affirmative issues
concerning special groups with peculiar problems. Whereas democracy has
provided the tool for addressing this issue in the mature federal democracies such as Canada and Switzerland, that of Nigeria seems to have been
complicated with the advent of oil as a strategic commodity. One of the
signs of a problematised federal system in Nigeria is seen in the character
of conflict generated by oil. It is not that oil in itself is evil, but problem
arises because of the attitude of the state towards its extraction and distribution of the wealth created by it. The preferences of dominant ethnicities that control the state (including a Nigerian military dominated Hausa-
Fulani with seeming collaboration of Ibos and Yoruba's in rulership) have
had their preferences reflected in the restructuring of the federation. This is
seen in the constitutional concentration of power at the federal government.
This tendency has made the system more ethnic driven and authoritarianian,
which then makes federalism a strange bed-fellow with democracy.

Literature tends to have essentially problematised federalism in Nigeria for its inability to effectively address the many issues of nation-building,
some of which are focused on in this study. Both fiscal imbalance and political underrepresentation have been identified as factors oiling the friction
in the federation (Uzodike and Fidelis, 2004). However, equitable representation and fiscal regimes are supposedly the natural outworking of the
principles of federalism and democracy (ibid.) Fiscal regimes, refers to the
existing asymmetrical relationship between the majority and the minority
ethnic groups in terms of the insensitive and systematic procurement and
transfer of financial resources from the territories of the minority ethnic
groups to the territories of the majority ethnic groups.

Societal variable of sociological forces of ethnic minority agitations of the Niger Delta reflects copiously in literature of federalism and democracy in Nigeria. Some scholars see ethnic minorities in Nigeria not in terms of numerical calculations but in terms of their socio-economic and political disadvantages vis-à-vis the majority ethnic groups (Agbese, 2003:239).That is also the view in this paper. Although the minorities have interpreted the creation of states and local governments as mechanisms of domination and a strategy for increasing the economic and political advantages of the majority ethnic groups, it has also created problems for democracy in terms of the character of politicians it breeds. Political elites are attracted by the oil wealth that comes effortlessly to the state or governments, but federal democracy does not seem to adequately address the political and economic needs of the masses of the ethnic minorities where oil is extracted. While there seems to be a consensus among political elites on the mismanagement of allocated resources of the governments, the masses or rural people of the oil producing regions have become essentially resistant and confrontational to the state and her cronies.

## 3.3. Oil and democracy in Nigeria: A resource war analysis

The thinking that wars and other violent conflicts in the 21$^{st}$ century will be about natural resources is difficult to refute, given instances of cases around the world, especially in Africa (Collier and Hoeffler, 1998: 568; Mwanasali, 2000: 145; De Soysa, 2000: 123). Nigeria, in the heat generated over oil extraction and distribution of its wealth, represents a typology of the resource war. In this war, institutional and behavioural designs as well as general performance of regimes are all shaped by the economies of the war. The trend of restructuring the federal system, activities of its constituent ethnological units and other sociological forces has been constitutive part of the strategic elements in the war. Between the oil producing communities of the Niger Delta, the federal government and oil companies, actors in the war are easily discernable. However, there exist gray areas in locating the major actors when it comes to identifying local enemies (internal colonialists) in this war. It is absolutely difficult figuring out which politician is really on the side of the mass of citizens since all politicians at the state and local government levels appear to be on the other side of the divide against the people, at least from 1999 to date. For the most part, it can be argued that the resistance in the Niger Delta region is part of the struggle to have a good share of revenue accruing from oil extraction. The repressiveness of the state towards threats to the continuous extraction of the oil and the struggle to occupy government house, whether at the local, state or federal government level by politicians is also part of this whole war for the oil resource, since currently, without the oil the state will collapse. It is oil that funds the state.

To this end, it is of significance to argue that liberal democracy is a key element in this war. Liberal democracy, in recent times, does not only claim rights over the oil, it sustains the authoritarianism and repressiveness of the state that oils the friction. The open secret is the conspiracy of political elites over the final beneficiaries of the oil wealth. That is the crux of the matter: Is oil oiling the friction?

There are many ways in which oil in Nigeria threatens democracy. To understand how, it is important to clear some gray areas in the conceptuali-sation of democracy and its desirability.

Apparently, liberalism in Nigeria is mutually antagonistic to democracy at many fronts, especially in terms of its inability to offer opportunities for resolution of conflicts through nonviolent means as well as its inability to allow a change of leadership through fair and free elections void of vio-lence. Liberal democracy guarantees minimal political rights to citizens, enough only to vote during elections but excluded from the day to day governance at the public realm. An alternative model of democracy, de-velopmental democracy, is human centred, and it considers the economic and social rights of citizens in addition to their political rights. According to Stokes (op.cit.38) development democracy provides new "types of so-cial and economic rights [with the] aims to facilitate greater participation. Yet, the recognition of new rights can be extended to other spheres such as cultural and ecological rights." It is the developmental concern embedded in the liberal economic and political processes of the Nigerian system that runs democracy dry.

Three ways in which oil threatens democracy in Nigeria are: its mode of extraction and distribution of its revenue; faulty federal structure and undevelopmental liberal political system.

Ecological consequences of oil extraction and distribution of the revenue derived have been predominantly negative for the democratic and economic aspirations of the oil producing communities. It is worth noting that Nigeria, as an oil producing country, became so pronounced in the 1970s. The state dominates the oil sector but actual exploration and refining are done by multinational corporations. This has implications for the autonomy of the state over the oil industry, in terms of regulating the activities of the oil companies. Besides, the state, more or less, plays the role of collecting and distributing of rents. In more than four decades Nigeria has earned about $340 billion dollars. Sadly, over 70% of Nigerians, especially of the oil producing regions, are still living in poverty (Obi, 2004).

Although discontents by the oil producing communities of the Niger Delta region over environmental degradation from oil exploration activities of oil companies was not a threat to the government and the oil companies in the 1980s, the situation changed in the 1990s with the uprising of the Ogonis against the then military regime. The Ogoni incidence helped in the demand for democracy in Nigeria, as the response of the state under General Sani Abacha incurred for itself a pariah status, disconnected from other democracies in the committee of nations. According to Steyn (2003) the Ogoni struggle is about oil related state of underdevelopment and environmental destruction:

But more importantly their struggle triggered the explosion of popular discontent amongst most of the other oil-producing ethnic minority communities residing in the Niger Delta, which discontent has plunged the whole region into political instability in recent years, thereby threatening the very basis of the Nigerian economy. This in itself is no small achievement for an ethnic minority group which, despite political, economic, social and environmental marginalisation dating back decades, took the political initiative to confront the powerful oil industry and their country's despotic military rulers. In the light of their successes (and failures) and the snowball effect of their struggle, the Ogoni struggle remains one of the most interesting and noteworthy case studies of contemporary oil-related ethnic minority environmental struggles in the developing world.

Having suffered destruction of traditional means of livelihood as a result of oil exploration since 1958, the Ogoni activism was meant to persuade Shell and the federal government of the need for them to pay constructive attention to the plight of the Ogonis. The degree of environmental consequences of oil extraction in Ogoniland and other parts of the Niger Delta region have been well documented (See Oil Watch, Human Rights Watch and Environmental Rights Action, 2004). The spill-over effect of the Ogoni demand for protection of their environment is seen in the transformation of this demand for the protection of the environment and quest for development into a militant articulation of development reflecting in the activities of some irregular armed groups today in the rest of the Niger Delta. The militancy of the youths in the region as a direct result of damage to the environment and its consequent loss of livelihoods as a result of oil exploration is captured by Ibeanu (2000) in "Oiling the Friction: Environmental conflict management in the Niger Delta, Nigeria." Apparently, the central issue in the management of conflict between the Ogonis, oil companies and the state in Nigeria is the environmental consequences of oil extraction. There is hardly any contest with regard to this from the mass of citizens affected negatively by oil extraction. However, the bulk of the political elites, who seem to co-operate in corruption whether from the north of Nigeria (Hausa-Fulani), west of the country (Yorubas), or eastern part of Nigeria (Ibos), can explain the resource war away by emphasising economic goals characteristics of the liberal economic and political processes.

Local opposition to the oil industry, perhaps for its perceived negative effect on the environment and livelihoods of the people in the Niger Delta, can be traced to historical era of colonialism in Nigeria, when rural peoples of the Okigwe and Owerri Divisions took up arms against oil exploration activities of Shell BP in the 1940s and 1950s (Steyn, Op.cit.). They did not only stop Shell-BP from entering their communities, they destroyed its equipment as well. Thereafter, on a general note, oil producing communities in the Niger Delta sued oil companies for pollution and loss of their lands when production of oil in large scale commenced in 1958. It appeared that the legal route was the most preferred method of addressing the grievances of local oil communities, with the exception of the declaration of the Republic of Niger Delta by Isaac Boro, Sam Owunaro and Nottingham Dick in 1967. The 1980s up to the 1990s and now have seen a transformation of that legal approach to a militant approached started by the Ogonis. Today, democracy is yet to address these grievances satisfactorily, institutionally and behaviourally since liberal democracy is part of a project towards winning the war for the oil resource, exemplified in the struggle of the major ethnic groups to control the federal government. It is also seen in a recent protest by some northern federal law makers over a law that guarantees oil producing areas access to revenue accruing from off-shore oil exploration and extraction.

The economy of the resource war, which involves irregular armed groups doing illegal trade in bunkering, the federal government, political elites, multinational oil companies and international partners, did not cause the war, but it is a major sustaining factor of the resource war (Ikelegbe, A, 2005: 208).

Politicians seeking elective positions, at the local and state government levels, do so because of recent attraction of federal allocations accruing from oil; personal ambitions of using the state as an instrument for accumulation of wealth. Thus, the oil that funds the state in the real sense funds the corrupt ambitions of politicians. This has increased value for political offices, for which contest and competition has become deadly. What are missing in the current democracy are predominantly character and right values in regard to practice that considers citizens as the object of politics and policy.

## 3.4. References

Collier, P. and Hoeffler, A. 1998. "On Economic Causes of Wars Driven by Rapacity or Paucity". M. Berdal and D.M. Malone eds. *Greed and Grievance: Economic Agenda in Civil Wars*, Boulder: Lynne Rienner.

Collier, P. and Hoeffler, A. 2001. *Greed and Grievance in Civil War*. Washington D.C.: World Bank Research Group.

De Soysa 2000. "The Resource Curse: Are Civil Wars Driven by rapacity or paucity," M.

Berdal and D.M. Malone eds.*Greed and Grievance: Economic Agenda in Civil Wars*, Boulder: Lynne Rienner

Diskin, A., Diskin, H., and Hazan, R.Y. 2005. "Why Democracies Collapse: The Reasons for Democratic Failure and Success" International Political Science Review, Volume 26 Number 3, July

Jinadu, L. 1979. "A Note on the Theory of Federalism" in Akiyemi, A.B. etal eds. *Readings on Federalism*, Lagos: Nigerian Institute of International Affairs

Ibeanu, O. 2000. "Oiling the Friction: Environmental Conflict Management in the Niger Delta, Nigeria." *Environmental Change & Security Project Report,* Issue 6

Ihonvbere, J.O. 2003. "The Nigerian State As an Obstacle to Federalism: To-wards A New Constitutional Compact for Democratic Politics" Gana, A.T. and Egwu, S.G. eds. *Federalism in Africa,* Volume Two, Trenton: Africa World Press

Ikelegbe, A. 2005. "The Economy of Conflict in the Oil Rich Niger Delta Region of Nigeria" Nordic*Journal of African Studies* 14(2)

Momoh, A.2003. "Civil Society and the Politics of Federalism in Nigeria" Gana T. A and Egwu, S.G. eds. *Federalism in Africa,* Volume Two, Trenton: Africa World Press

Obi, C. 2004. "Nigeria: democracy on trial" Text of Lecture organized by the Swedish Development Forum, Stockholm, Tuesday, September 14

Steyn, S. M. 2003. "Oil politics in Ecuador and Nigeria: a perspective from Environmental history y on the struggles between Ethnic minority groups, multinational oil Companies and national governments," Being a Doctoral Dissertation submitted to the faculty of humanities (Department of History) at the University of the Free State Bloemfontein, South Africa

Stokes, G.2001. "Democracy and Citizenship" Carter, A. and Stokes, G eds. *Democratic Theory Today,* U.K: Blackwell Publishers Inc.

Nwandasali, M. 2000. "The view from below." M. Berdal and D.M. Malone eds.*Greed and Grievance: Economic Agenda in Civil Wars Boulder*, Boulder: Lynne Rienner.

# 4. Politicisation and underdevelopment of the Niger Delta Region

Dr. Francis George Umukoro

↗ POLITICAL THEORY

## Abstract

*This chapter explores the trends of the Niger Delta crisis within the context of political theory. It explains the crisis in the region and proffers strategic options for resolution. The principal thesis of this paper is focused on the root cause of the Niger Delta crisis which is traceable to the failure of the political class to address the needs of the citizens in the region. Prominent among which is the provision of basic amenities necessary for the well being of the inhabitants of the region bearing in mind that this region provides the economic mainstay for the whole country for the five decades.*

## 4.1. Introduction

Poverty of development has been a major theme in virtually all the attempts made at explaining the situations in the Niger Delta region. Most of the contending perspectives have also been focused on the politics of oil exploitation between the Nigerian State, local communities and the oil multinationals. Issues such as negligence, environmental degradation and economic exploitation of oil producing communities have featured prominently but adequate fairness has not been extended to dynamics of political theory and its attendant effects on underdevelopment of the Niger Delta. The objective of this paper therefore is to take a cursory look at the nature of the conspiracy of the political class and examine the attendant effects of their activities on the problems associated with the underdevelopment of the Niger Delta.

## 4.2. Poverty in the Niger Delta

It is an indisputable fact that there are significant differences in the development of the various areas in Nigeria. However, the existence of massive poverty in the Niger Delta and the incredible wealth in the region is potentially destabilising. One fundamental question that needs to be asked is whether it is justifiable to deprive a set of people the opportunities offered by civilisation? Providing solution to this question can be achieved if we can appreciate the fact that the dynamics of global stability is to ensure a future where all humankind would be given the opportunity to freely associate and create initiatives to making the world a better place for all. It is perhaps relevant to point out here that countries worldwide have developed a belief at eliminating poverty completely and also develop all aspects of the individual to start a process of commitment to social aspirations and attainment of national goals.

Human beings grow through several stages. At one time or the other they encounter poverty in certain areas of their lives, but as Martin Luther, King (Jnr) did posit, "the ultimate measure of a man is not when he finds himself in a moment of comfort and convenience but when he stands at a time of challenge and controversy." Therefore, it should be understood that no condition is permanent. The poor of today might be the rich of tomorrow since the world is dynamic. The World Bank's clarification of poverty is that; poverty is hunger. Poverty is lack of shelter. Poverty is being sick and not being able to see a doctor. Poverty is not being able to go to school and not knowing how to read. Poverty is not having a job, is fear for the future, living one day at a time. Poverty is losing a child to illness brought about by unclean water. Poverty is powerlessness, lack of representation and freedom. Therefore, it is not an understatement to say that poverty has many faces, which it changes from place to place and across time, and that it has been described in many ways. Most often, poverty is a situation every human being wants to escape. So, the existence of poverty in any community is a call to action for the poor and wealthy alike. A call to change the world so that many more may have enough to eat, have adequate shelter, have access to education and healthcare facilities, have protection from violence, and have a voice in what happens in their communities. Various studies on poverty have proven that it has many dimensions. Thus, poverty has to be viewed through a variety of indicators, and how such indicators are vulnerable to risks and of socio-political access.

## 4.3. Societal value of Nigerian political class

It is an incontrovertible fact that the central problem of man is economic and all other problems are secondary. It is within this context, perhaps, that Ake (2001) opined that man's first loyalty is to his economic interest and his secondary loyalty is to the organisations or institutions which serve to promote this interest. This implies that the sole justification of a state is the economic advantages which division of labour and exchange of goods and services can confer on the inhabitants of the state (Stanton, 1981). It should, therefore, be understood that families do not aggregate and unite in one community or state just for the love of one another. The compelling motivation is economic. Thus, if this motivation is taken away, the state becomes meaningless to an average citizen living in it. Giving credence to this framework is the conspiracy of a class over another as one gains the upper hand in the control of means of the factors of production.

Over the ages, the morality and values of the Nigerian society has tended to support the preservation of the existing division of labour and distribution of wealth. This is why there are clear difficulties in the area of wealth generation, distribution and management. It is, therefore, obvious that there exist a conspiracy by the political class against the ordinary Nigerian citizens in pursuit of the prime goal of primitive accumulation of wealth, which is a tradition that has become a societal value. This is irrespective of the location and ethnicity of the perpetrator. This conspiracy is responsible for the under-development of the people. The quest for power and wealth has forced many people to consider human relationship as secondary. This situation has given rise to inequality, and economic inequality by all intents and purposes will reproduce endless inequality. This postulation aptly describes the situations in the Niger Delta region of Nigeria.

Various studies have given credence to the above postulation as seen in the fact that those from the economically privileged groups tend to be better educated, are more cultured, have higher social status, and are more successful professionally and politically. Those who are economically privileged tend to be interested in preserving the existing social order and those who are disadvantaged by the order, particularly its distribution of wealth, have a strong interest in changing the social order, particularly its nature of wealth distribution.

## 4.4.  A Review of the Niger Delta Crisis

The Niger Delta region of Nigeria is made of nine states located in the south-south part of the county. These are Abia, Akwa-Ibom, Bayelsa, Cross-River, Delta, Edo, Imo, Ondo and River states. This is a region endowed with abundant oil deposit and it accounts for the reason why Nigeria is the fifth largest supplier of crude oil in the world. Nigeria, with a population of about 140 million people is made up of 36 states with the Niger Delta region accounting for an estimated population of about 30 million people scattered in 75,000 km$^2$ land mass.

However, within the last two decades, issues about the Niger Delta have attracted attentions in many areas of discussions as a result of the changing politics of oil exploitation in the region. The region has been characterised by increasing spate of insecurity and threats capable of dislocating the corporate existence of Nigeria. Series of uprisings have been taken place most of which have been suppressed. Notwithstanding this suppression, the region has not witnessed peace compared to other parts of the country. Some remarkable academic inquiries into the changing face of the crisis in the Niger Delta indicate that the crisis reveals the unfortunate legacy of global capitalism. This view was shared by Ibeanu (2003), who pointed out that the Niger Delta conflict conceals more than it reveals. Similarly, Imobighe (2005) on his part identifies a common denominator to the persistent conflicts in the region. He opined that whether one talks about the conflicts between the various communities and the oil companies, or conflicts between the various communities and relevant authorities, it will be found that they are all predicated on one single denominator: the activities of the political class and multinational oil companies. In other words, the problem in the Niger Delta is hinged on the fact that the people's major sources of livelihood, land and water have been adversely affected by government policies and the operations of the oil companies. The summary of these opinions is the problem associated with wealth, the resource curse and the complex series of connection between unemployment and youth violence. The crisis is a problem of wealth because the region which is richly bless with large deposit of crude oil, which contributes about 2.6 million barrels of oil per day and over 87% of Nigeria's annual export earning still records a high incidence of poverty.

It is important at this point to state that the regime of crises in the Niger Delta has expanded from oil to include ethnic conflicts, communal conflicts, and environmental crisis. A checklist of the security challenge that emerged from these activities presented by Omoweh (2003) include the challenge of poverty alleviation and deprivations (L1); the challenge of human and infrastructural development (L2); the challenge of confidence building between the various stake holders within the region (L3); the challenge of environmental pollution and ecological degradations that accompany oil exploration and exploitation (L4); the activities of migrant oil workers that generate threats to social harmony (L5); the challenge of reaching a fair system of resource allocation in the country (L6); the incidence of hostage taking and propensity to armed insurrections within the region (L7); the use of the youth by some members of the political elites in the electoral bargaining (L8), and the discouraging level of corporate social responsibility by major profiteers within the region (L9). All these create serious distractions from the need to give enabling environment for economic and social development.

## 4.5. The political dimension

It is important to note at this stage that unlike the logics of contract given by great political scientists like Hobbes, Locke and Rousseau, there was no case of contract with regard to the evolution of the Nigerian state. Rather, Nigeria was a product of colonial conquest, a rather ambitious attempt at political cloning. Consequently, what exists today as Nigeria is the fallout of imperial adventure which coerced alien geopolitical entities into a nation-state. The situation is compounded by the narrow ambitions of members of the country's political class who, since independence in 1960, have preferred to attain and exploit political power for parochial rather than national interests. It is equally important to restate that none of the three major Nigerian tribes – Igbo, Yoruba, and the Hausa-Fulani – that consistently contest and occupy key political offices since independence contributes to the national wealth like the minorities of the Niger Delta. The situation is compounded by the existence of indigenous exploiters from the region that benefit from the status quo ante and collaborate with alien exploiters to perpetuate the adverse human living condition in the Niger Delta.

The problem, however, takes its root from the fact that the region that provides the wealth of the nation is seriously impoverished with the bulk of the indigenous inhabitants alienated from their means of livelihood and the evident wealth that accrue from their domain. This scenario has been variously identified as the source of the grievances that culminated in the persistent assaults on the state. Onyeoziri (2004) summed it when he argued that the denial of access to positions of power and privilege for people of this region by the federal government contributed to the emergence of tensions within the region. Thus, this exclusion from such privileges and power brings a lot of ill-feelings. The resultant effect is the intensification of frustrations that now compels the people of Niger Delta to challenge the legitimacy of the political structures in Nigeria.

## 4.6. Activities of the political class

Closely related to the issues discussed above are the situations of visible signs of discomfort like the basic issues of state life, namely generation, management and distribution of resources as they related to its political and social life. The Nigerian political circumstance which brought into focus the problems of the Niger Delta began in the 1950s. Between 1900 and 1950 the unfair and unacceptable distinction between majority and minority ethnic groups had not yet risen. However, the political culture profile of Nigeria changed dramatically from about 1954 with the introduction of regionalism. In each of the three regions that made up Nigeria – North, East and West – the dominant culture groups cultivated a sense of numerical population superiority that became pronounced during the struggle for independence. This quest for dominance by the major ethnic groups was at the expense of development and healthy progress of all parts of the nation. Thus, the f failure to achieve any reasonable measure of economic growth contributed to the emergence of contradictions and consciousness in the country's socio-economic formations.

At the beginning of 1954, the nature of politics in the Nigerian polity extravagantly defied cherished norms of development. Everything was literally reduced to politics, laden with disproportional emotion. Those who benefited from the system consistently mobilised all ethnic, economic and political apparatus at their disposal to under develop the nation. As the situation unfolded and constituted, the state became an instrument used by the dominant and powerful in the economy to protect and reproduce the existing property and power relations. Invariably, it involved the regression of the economic and social classes whose interests and development were antagonistically opposed to the existing property and power relations. In this circumstance, the state, with its capitalist orientation, ensured that private interests, foreign and local, were richer than the state or government and it became impossible for them to meet the basic needs of the civil society and people as regards food, clothing, shelter, health, education, transportation, and housing.

The political class therefore saddled themselves with the responsibility of discountenancing the interest of the people and to harness all available instruments and opportunity to divide the people and set them against each other. This circumstance explains the activities in public, of Nigerian political parties which rested greatly on invested ethnic and social sentiments. The fears of the minority ethnic group in all the regions were rooted in the colonial states publics and the capitalist tendencies it acquired. The overwhelming numerical strength of the major ethnic groups, especially in the Niger Delta, denied the minority groups access to state power, adequate political representation and basic social services.

These fears gave rise to the agitation for creation of minority ethnic states, and a barrage of protests led to the setting up of a commission in 1958. The commission, among others, recommended that in order to allay the fears of the people, a Special Development Commission be set up to oversee the development of the Niger Delta given its peculiar ecology, level of backwardness and its minority status in the federation. But the large amount of politics in the polity was a setback to any meaningful progress. Agitation for state creation was proposed on the bases of linguistic and ethnic determination. This premise, to all intents and purposes, was myopic. The Action Group (AG), a political party with stronghold in the western region of Nigeria, was the chief architect of the proposal for the creation of states on ethnic and linguistic bases. Its initial support for the creation of mid-west region was to argue for the return of Ilorin (an emirate in the North) to the west of Nigeria. The AG's posture was conceived as an instrument to devastate the northern hegemony.

53

On the other hand, the North opposed the adoption of state creation on minority ethnic bases. However, it saw the opportunity in the west and east of Nigeria to destabilise the National Council of Nigeria and the Cameroons (NCNC), which was a strong political party that had strong roots in the east and west, and the AG. But, in order to contain the spread of the Northern People's Congress, in their traditional spheres of influence, other major parties adopted the strategy of exposing the insincerity of the NPC (a strong northern political party) and promising the ethnic minorities their right to self-determination. This strategy made the Rivers State Movement to announce the suspension of its agitation for a separate Rivers State from the east in August 1964.

The sum total of it all is that, by the end of the First Republic, it was visibly clear that the major ethnic groups and their political parties were only interested in the activities of the state movements to the extent that it enhanced their chances for the control of the centre.

The military, however, came into the political arena through a coup. And, throughout the military era, there was visibly no improvement in the life of the people of the Niger Delta. What they rather got was rough bargains in the class politics of the military-cum-civilians in government. The return to civil rule in 1999 offered hope, but rather than hope visiting the communities in the Niger Delta, despair and hopelessness have been the lot of the people of the Niger Delta.

The conspiracy of the political class continued in feeding fat on oil from the Niger Delta. The conspiracy this time around is total as local collaborations within the same class bracket, deceived their people in the name of governance to pauperise them. Rather than argue credibly for development, the governors of the states in the Niger Delta region, the chairmen of the third tier of government, and the political appointees from the Niger Delta wallowed far in ill-gotten wealth, and this situation further dichotomised the people and demonised them by arming the youth and cult groups.

At the federal level, too much politics continued and legislators toyed with the idea of revenue re-formalisation by paying lip services to alleviating the poverty of the land. As they funded the agencies set up for developmental purpose, they returned the other way to collect it back and the status quo remains. Unnecessary conferences and seminars that culminate in the all-time money wasting exercises were held not to alleviate poverty but to intensify the debate on nothingness.

In order to give credence to the preceding discussions, efforts are made in this study to carry out some empirical analysis useful for substantiating the points raised in the discussions. Thus, two hypotheses derived from the discussions given.

## 4.7. Hypotheses of the study

The preceding discussions can be hypothesised in two distinctive statements. And, it is on these hypotheses that data collected from selected respondents were analysed.

The first hypothesis states that:
– The political class has not worsened the expected level of development as exemplified by their activities.

The second hypothesis states that:
– The political class has contributed immensely to the reduction of poverty as exemplified by their activities.

## 4.8. Sample and Data

Twenty (20) associates of the supposedly elected members of the Federal Houses of Assembly and ten (10) associates of the supposedly elected members of Houses of Assembly in the Niger Delta region were selected for this study. In addition, twenty (20) students currently undergoing various degree courses in universities located in the Niger Delta region were included in the sample.

Data were gathered only through structured interviews. This was to allow for extensive discussions that took place within seven months.

## 4.9. Variables and measures

The dependent variable for this study is poverty. Poverty was measured using the World Bank's clarification of poverty, which are: hunger, lack of shelter, being sick and not being able to see a doctor, not being able to go

to school, not having a job, fear for the future, lack of representation and freedom. These indicators are summarised as follows:
- (P1) education
- (P2) food
- (P3) shelter
- (P4) job

The independent variables are represented by the different facets of the political class. These are itemised as follows:
- (C1) oil bunkerers
- (C2) legislators
- (C3) executives
- (C4) judiciary

In the analysis of the second hypothesis, the activities of the political class are classified as follows:
- (L1) the challenge of poverty alleviation and deprivations
- (l2) the challenge of human and infrastructural development
- (L3) the challenge of confidence building between the various stake holders within the region
- (L4) the challenge of environmental pollution and ecological degradations that accompany oil exploration and exploitation
- (L5) the activities of migrant oil workers that generate threats to social harmony
- (L6) the challenge of reaching a fair system of resource allocation in the country
- (L7) the incidence of hostage taking and propensity to armed insurrections within the region
- (L8) the use of the youth by some members of the political elites in the electoral bargaining
- (L9) the discouraging level of corporate social responsibility by major profiteers within the region

## 4.10. Data Analysis

The following coefficients determining the relationships between variables were recorded by applying the statistical correlation ($r$) to the set of data collected.

**Table 1: Impact of political class on types of poverty**

| Variable | C1<br>Oil bunkers | C2<br>Legislators | C3<br>Executives | C4<br>Judiciary |
|---|---|---|---|---|
| P1<br>Education | 0.54 | 0.48 | 0.42 | 0.03 |
| P2<br>Food | 0.42 | 0.41 | 0.33 | 0.01 |
| P3<br>Shelter | 0.52 | 0.42 | 0.31 | 0.03 |
| P4<br>Job | 0.47 | 0.40 | 0.42 | 0.01 |

*$P<0.01$, **$p< 0.05$

**Table 2: Relationship between the activities of the political class and types of poverty**

| Variable | 1 | 2 | 3 | 4 | 5 | 6 | 7 | 8 | 9 |
|---|---|---|---|---|---|---|---|---|---|
| P1<br>Education | 43 | 31 | 31 | 42 | 40 | 39 | 28 | 44 | 30 |
| P2<br>Food | 42 | 31 | 30 | 44 | 13 | 29 | 28 | 34 | 31 |
| P3<br>Shelter | 41 | 40 | 37 | 31 | 30 | 28 | 17 | 32 | 21 |

*$p< 0.01$, ** $p < 0.05$

## 4.11. Results and discussions

The activities of the political class in area of oil bunkering are quite over-whelming as table 1 shows. With a correlation coefficient value of r =0.54 it is obvious that the political class were only interested in their personal wealth acquisition at the expense of educational development. This is closely indicated with the coefficient value of r =0.52 on shelter, 0.47 on lack of job, and 0.42 on non-availability of food for the people.

Similarly, activities of the political class in the area of legislation displayed a high level of correlation with the impact on non-educational development having a higher impact (r = 0.48), while others had closer coefficients.

The political class in the area of executives were also not left out in this circumstance. Education was also highly affected with coefficient value of r = 0.42, while shelter recorded a low value of r = 0.31.

Political class in the area of judiciary had the lowest impact on poverty items. Education and shelter, however top the list with r = 0.03 respectively, while food and job had r = 0.01 also.

From table 2, activities of the political class arising from what they support and its respective impact on the four variables of poverty were presented.

Lack of effective contribution to poverty alleviation on the four variables accounted for the highest levels of impact comparatively. For example, lack of contribution to poverty alleviation resulted in a 43% impact on declining level of education, 42% on lack of food, and 39% on lack of job.

Similarly, the use of the youth for political activities accounted also for a substantial amount of impact on the four variables of poverty. Notable among these are the impact on education and job with 44% and 40% respectively. However, lack of social responsibility on the part of the multinational occasioned by the influence of the political class accounted for a moderate impact on the four variables of poverty.

## 4.12. Strategic options to resolution

Although confrontation as suggested by many concerned Nigerians has top the list of strategic options, this study believed that one principal way to address the Niger Delta question is to first address the root causes of the vicious cycle of frustrations in the region. To this effect, this paper proposes the following prescriptions:

– Concerted efforts must be made to alleviate and, probably, eradicate the incidence of poverty in the region. This is because poverty as is the parent of crime and revolution.

- The activities of the Niger Delta Development Corporation (NDDC) must be boosted to address the fundamental needs of the various communities and peoples within the regions. If this recommendation is already in place, then it should be intensified.
- There is the need to create more employment opportunities for indigenes of the region. It must, however, be realised that genuine investment inflows which can generate such employment opportunities cannot materialise in an atmosphere of armed conflicts, hostage taking and general insecurity. By implication, the people of the Niger Delta have to contribute to the process by ensuring that the prerequisite peaceful atmosphere for development is guaranteed in the region.
- The various corporate agencies in general, and oil multinationals in particular, should also enhance their commitments to the discharge of corporate social responsibility programmes to their host communities.
- The government through its various security agencies should also make concerted efforts at halting the proliferation of small arms and light weapons in the region. In particular, the local political elites must shun violence and use of armed youth groups to harass and intimidate political opponents. This is because; such actions support the cultivation of a culture of violence in the society.
- The criminal activities of oil bunkerers must be checked as they contribute in fueling the conflicts in the region. The major profiteers from the bunkering business appropriate from creating phony war zones to engage the military elsewhere to and create room for then- bunkering activities. It is unfortunate that many of the youths being used by bunkerers to make trouble are ignorant of this reality.
- There must also be concerted efforts to arrive at realistic revenue allocation formula in the country, which will accommodate the challenges from the region. This is because the question of revenue allocation remains central to agitations from the Niger Delta. However, it must be realised that increment in revenue may not be the solution as this can stimulate further greed and official corruption as well as increase political violence associated with the quest for state power in the region.
- There is also a need to address the issues associated with the allocation of oil blocs in the country. This will require an amendment of existing laws to give communities and states equity stake-holding in oil and gas

exploration. Revenue accruing from this should be administered by trust funds, with 50 per cent used for urgent infrastructure needs and the remaining saved for the future.

- It is also the position of the paper that the activities of missionary organisations which extol the virtues of peace and forgiveness should be encouraged; if for nothing else, they will help to ensure that the aggrieved indigenes and other inhabitants of the region will appreciate.
- Finally, concerted efforts should be made to revive the ailing educational systems. Government and the people through their representatives should come together to save the future of the younger generation from drifting into acts of terrorism arising from lack of reasonable educational system. This can best be achieved by building more schools and ensuring that no fee is charged for pupils in primary and secondary schools.

It is assumed that these measures will require and elicit a participatory and people oriented approach to solving the problem and also helping in lessening the tensions, agitation and perceptions of unfairness, while guaranteeing poverty alleviation through necessary developmental activities in the Niger Delta.

## 4.13. Conclusion

The Niger Delta has gotten into where it is today because of the nature of our Nigerian politics and the fact that the role of oil is multi-layered and complex. It involves very high stakes, conferring immense wealth upon those who capture state power or are directly connected to it. It acts as a lubricant for the cohesion and reproduction of the dominant socio-economic system, while acting as cementing agent for the highly traditionalized Nigerian hegemonic elite.

A man can contribute to the development of the society according to his ability only if he is in a fit position, physically and mentally to do so.

## 4.14. References

Ake C (2001) *Democracy and Development in Africa* Spectrum Books Ltd. Ibadan
Ibeanu O., (2003) *The Proliferation of Small Arms and Light Weapons in the Niger Delta: An Introduction* p. 40

Imobighe,T (2005) quoted in Nnamdi K. Obasi, "The Military and Management of Conflicts in the Niger Delta" in Amos G. Adedeji and Istafanus S. Zabadi (eds.) *The Military and Management of Internal Conflicts in Nigeria* (Abuja: National War College, 2005) p. 114

Omoweh, D.A. (2003) Oil and Politics of Environmental Degradation in the Niger Delta of Nigeria: A Historical Perspective In Akinyeye Y. (ed.) *Nigeria and the Wider World in the 20*[th]*. Century* pp. 180-200

Onyeoziri F. (2004) *Alternative Policy Options for Managing National Questions in Nigeria.* John Archers, Ibadan p. 47

Stanton, W.J (1981) *Fundamentals of Marketing* 6th. ed. McGraw-hill

# 5. Development interventions of oil multinationals in Nigeria's Niger Delta: for the rich or the poor?

Mathew I. Eboreime and Douglaston G. Omotor

## Abstract

*The conflict in the Niger Delta is significantly correlated with the problem of increasing depletion of infrastructural resources attributable to severe environmental degradation and other social costs unleashed on oil producing communities. To ameliorate these negative externalities, oil multinational companies have been involved in various community development interventions. However, scepticism still persists as to whether the core poor really benefits from such interventions. This study applied a simple statistical technique to evaluate the appropriateness of these interventions and also comparatively analysed the performance of two major multinational oil companies (Shell and Agip) which operate in the region. The findings revealed that the interventions were targeted at the richer minority, and Shell was worse, relatively speaking, in their development interventions.*

## 5.1. Introduction

One of the cardinal objectives of the Millennium Development Goals (MDGs) is poverty eradication. Issues of poverty also constitute a major discourse in contemporary development economics. In Nigeria, the problem of poverty is very worrisome not only to the individuals, but organisations and governments at various levels have over the years put in place various interventions to alleviate it. It is estimated that about sixty-five million Nigerians, approximately half the size of the country's population, live below poverty line of US$1 per day (Thisday, 2006). Earlier statistics indicate that the incidence of poverty is also on the rise in Nigeria as the population of the moderately poor, for instance, rose from 21 per cent in 1980 to 36 per cent in 1996 while the percentage of the core poor more than quadrupled over the same period (FOS in United Nations, 2001).

Ostensibly, the Niger Delta region is worst hit by the poverty endemic (Omotor, 2009). According to Omene (2003), the deltaic region is the least developed region in Nigeria with its per capita income below the national average of $280. Other than systemic factors that aggravate the incidence of poverty nationally, the Niger Delta area is further impoverished in a very significant way by the negative externalities associated with crude oil exploration and production.

The activities of multinational oil firms have been characterised by severe environmental problems in host communities. These include the physical alienation of scarce agricultural land by oil exploration and production companies; the flaring of over 70 per cent of associated gas, which causes acid rain, reduces soil fertility, pollutes sources of drinking water, incorporates carcinogens into both marine and aquatic food chains, generates intense heat and perpetually banish night in many host communities; fishery decline; biodiversity loss; delta forest loss and land degradation. Frequent oil spillage has also been reported as a major cause of decline in agricultural production and increase in health problems attributable to oil industry activities (see Shell 2000, Nyemutu Robert 1998, Obi 1997 and Ikein 1990).

The above problems have increased poverty incidences, severe impoverishment, unemployment, youth restiveness and militancy, conflicts over land compensations and displacement in oil producing areas. In response to increasing community agitation and conflicts, the multinational oil companies embarked on various development interventions (projects/programmes) to alleviate poverty in host communities. Some of the projects include provision of social infrastructure, micro credit, bursary awards and scholarships. This, notwithstanding, there is a serious concern as to which of the socio-economic groups benefits more from the development interventions of oil multinationals (the rich or the poor?). Do the bulk of economic empowerment benefits go to the richer class in the society? Providing an answer to this question necessitates the need to evaluate the degree to which oil multinationals in the Niger Delta of Nigeria deliberately target the core poor in their project designs and interventions. The rest of the paper is divided into five sections. Following the introduction, section 2 briefly reviews some literature on poverty while section 3 discusses the poverty trend of the Niger Delta of Nigeria. Section 4 presents the research design and method of study, while the results are discussed in section 5. Section 6 concludes the paper with some recommendations.

## 5.2. Brief review of the literature

Many economists believe that the income dimension of poverty remains the best approach to its definition despite several shortcomings. To this school of thought, people are said to be poor if their incomes fall below the minimum level necessary to meet the bare necessities of life (see Olaide and Essang 1975; Todaro 1972; Akpakpan 1991; and, Leftwich and Sharp 1980) and are such unable to meet the basic necessities of life. Nwosu (2000:210) conceptualised severe poverty as a direct consequence of unmet basic human needs and basic human rights. According to him, basic human needs are "mainly biophysical requirements for maintaining survival, namely, the amount of food, clean water, adequate shelter, access to health services, educational opportunities ... to which every person is entitled by virtue of being born." Poverty in this regard can generally be construed as transcending material deprivations such as low consumption and low income with adverse consequences on health and education among other human development anchors of the vulnerable, voiceless and powerless poor (World Bank, 2001; Wonacott and Wonacott, 1979; Ajakaiye and Adeyeye, 2001 and CASS 2004).

In the literature, various approaches have been adopted to target poverty or identify the poor before the commencement of specific development interventions aimed at uplifting the living conditions of the poor. One of such is the case of Grameen Bank in Bangladesh, a successful rural finance institution, whose eligibility criteria include the requirement that project beneficiaries should be from household with less than half an acre of land or with total assets not exceeding the value of one acre of land (Von Pischke, 1991). Another strategy generally applied to deter the rich from participating in poverty projects is to deliberately ensure that the loan size is very small (FINCA, 1996). The World Bank (1983) noted that useful definitions of the poor have often relied on an approximate identification of a target group such as small farmers, urban slum dwellers, or those lacking adequate water or access to primary school. Simple means tests have also been applied in several social programmes to identify the poor. This method, for example, has been used in the food stamp programmes in Jamaica, Honduras, Sri Lanka and Zambia. Also, sophisticated econometric techniques are available for determining eligibility for participation in poverty reduction interventions (see Grosh and Baker, 1995). However, in Nigeria, many so-called development interventions targeted at poverty reduction in oil producing communities apparently apply no specific identification criterion. Also, there have been articulated strategies in providing socio-economic empowerment for the poor. This paper attempts to fill some of these perceived gaps.

## 5.3. Research design and methodology

The literatures on an appropriate quantitative methodology for evaluating poverty targeting is mute; so, also are existing studies on comparative measurements of interventions as compared to the pre-intervention stage in Nigeria as earlier noted. Consequent upon this, this study employs an exploratory analysis to evaluate and compare interventions by oil multinational organizations in Nigeria.

Two multinational oil firms were chosen in this study, namely: the Nigeria Agip Oil Company Limited (Agip) and the Shell Petroleum Development Company Limited (Shell). They jointly produce over 50 per cent of Nigeria's annual crude oil output.

The study area for Agip covers several communities in seven upland locations of the companies at four of the major oil producing states of Nigeria – Bayelsa, Delta, Imo and Rivers. Frankly speaking, these states account for over 80 per cent of oil production in Nigeria. The communities are: For Agip[1]; Mgbede, Ebegoro, Oshie and Okposi (all in Rivers state). Others are: Biseni (Bayelsa), Akri (Imo) and Kwale (Delta). The study areas (states) for Shell[2] are: Enugbo – Abatu in Oguta (Imo), Mmahu (Imo), Obiakpu (Imo), Elele-Alumini (Rivers) and Owaza (Abia). A total of 140 respondents completed the questionnaire and 134 were found usable.

The sampling techniques used in the survey exercise include a combination of stratified, purposeful and simple random sampling. The question-

---

[1] The remarkable cooperation of Agip in the course of the field work, in terms of providing sample frame of project beneficiaries, arranging for meetings and providing logistic support made the survey exercise highly successful.
[2] There was deliberate refusal of Shell to cooperate during the field work. This is why only 22 project beneficiaries were sampled (see Eboreime 2007:144-156).

naire is the key source of information for this research. The survey data relate to 2006.

The analytical approach adopted involves the Chi-square technique (see McClave and Benson 1988: 1004-1007 and Sincich 1986: 778), contingency tables, graphical expositions and the first two measures of the Foster-Greer-Thorbecke class of poverty measures (See Prennushi *et al* 2002:405-407; and Grosh and Baker, 1995: 10).

Count data were collected to determine the relationship between two different methods of data classification; that is, per capita household expenditure versus standard level of living. The indicators or proxy variables of the former include: type of construction material, type of dwelling, sanitary practice and educational attainment. A statistical significant relationship between the classifications indicates that either the rich or the poor were targeted with project benefits. The reverse is for insignificant relationships.

## 5.4. Data presentation, analysis and discussion

Four levels of analyses were undertaken in this paper: the analysis of contingency tables using the Chi-square approach, percentage distributions, graphical expositions and the Foster-Greer-Thorbecke class of poverty measures.

The raw data in the Chi-square contingency tables for Nigerian Agip Oil Company are presented in Tables 1, 2, 3 and 4 as un-bracketed figures. These tables show the relationship between per capita household expenditure of different household categories and each of the four indicators of level of living. In Table 1, for instance, the calculated Chi-square ($q^{2)}$ value was neither statistically significant at the 5 per cent nor at 10 per cent level. This implies that there is no significant statistical relationship between the two classifications – per capital household expenditure and sanitary practice. In other words, project benefits were not specifically targeted at any income group. The outcomes of Tables 2, 3 and 4 are similar to that of Table 1 above.

Similarly, the Chi-square contingency tables for the Shell Petroleum Development Company are shown in Tables 5, 6, 7 and 8. The only classification that proved to be significant statistically is the classification between household per capita expenditure categories and type of construction materials indicator in Table 7. This shows that the Shell Petroleum targeted one of the income groups – in this case, the richer class. However, the other classification between household expenditures and living standard indicators in Tables 5, 6 and 8 were not statistically significant.

The next stage of the analysis involves the construction of the relevant percentage distributions for the raw data in the previous contingency tables and the associated graphical expositions. The relevant percentage distributions are found in Tables 1,2,3,4,5,6,7 and 8 as bracketed figures. For the Nigerian Agip Oil Company, the percentage distributions in Tables 1,2,3 and 4 clearly shows that the deviations of the various indicators of living standards are all closed to their expected percentage values, which means that Agip did not target any particular group in the distribution of project benefits.

Furthermore, the percentage distribution for Shell is shown as bracketed figures in Tables 5, 6, 7 and 8. Apart from Table 7 that shows significant deviation of the type "of construction material" variables from their expected values (meaning that one form or another of poverty targeting exist), other living standard indicators in Tables 5,6 and 8 show that the deviations from their expected value are insignificant (that is, no particular income groups was targeted with project benefits).

Additionally, the graphical analyses in Figures 1, 2, 3 and 4 (Agip) on the one hand, and Figures 5, 6, 7 and 8 (Shell) provide a visual amplification of the results in the tables of percentage distributions.

Finally, the first two measures of Foster-Greer-Thorbecke class of poverty measures (poverty headcount and poverty gap) were employed to shed more light on the issue of poverty targeting by both multinational oil companies (see Grosh and Baker 1995:10; Prennushi, Rudqvist and Subbarao, 2003:405-407). Agip and Shell have poverty headcount ratios of 0.16 and 0.32 respectively. Therefore, 32 per cent of Shell's beneficiaries were below the poverty line while that of Agip amounted to 16 per cent. With Shell having a poverty gap of 0.08 and Agip 0.03 respectively, the severity of poverty among project beneficiaries was greater for the former as compared to the later.

Given the outcomes of the above analyses as well as a careful qualitative overview, the two multinational oil firms – Agip and Shell – generally targeted project beneficiaries in the higher consumption category (rich) as opposed to those in the low consumption group (poor).

## 5.5. Summary and conclusion

The Niger Delta is one of the poorest regions in Nigeria. The activities of oil multinationals greatly aggravated and exacerbated the incidence of poverty due to the extensive destruction of the means of livelihood means of the indigenous population in fishery and farming. Thus, to curb severe impoverishment, youth restiveness and militancy in the region and secure the social license required for the hitch-free oil production activities, oil firms launched various programmes with the aim of raising the living standard of the people. However, the research results in this paper clearly show that the bulk of these project benefits went to the richer class in the society, while the core poor benefited in relatively marginal ways.

The above result is corroborated by the observation of Daukoru (2004:81) in discussing the pre-disposing factors to the Niger Delta Community Crisis. In his words, "after all these years, there is hardly a thriving oil company (ies) – led agro – program with the capacity to keep the youths busy: fish ponds, rice farms and others are easily abandoned. The few advertised successes are one – man schemes for older folks and do not really address the key problem of youth violence."

Thus, as a way forward in resolving the endemic problem of poverty in the region and to reduce the spate of violence and armed struggle among the local people, multinational oil companies should re – strategise their community development initiatives in such a manner as to channel the bulk of project benefits to the bottom 30 per cent of the local population.

**Table 1 Evaluating Poverty Targeting – Raw Data and Percentage Distribution by Per Capita Household Expenditure and Sanitary Practice (Agip)**

| (N) | | Sanitary Practice | | | Totals |
|---|---|---|---|---|---|
| | | Flush Toilet | Covered Pit | Open Air | |
| Per capita Household Expenditure | 18,000-47,999(low) | 3 (14) | 9 (41) | 10 (45) | 22 (100) |
| | 48,000-99,999 (average) | 19 (33) | 18 (31) | 21 (36) | 58 (100) |
| | 100,000-above (high) | 16 (30) | 21 (39) | 17 (31) | 54 (100) |
| Totals | | 38 (28) | 48 (36) | 48 (36) | 134 (100) |

Calculated $x^2$: 3.637, Critical values of $x^2$: $x^2_{.05} = 9.488$, $x^2_{.10} = 7.779$

**Table 2 Evaluating Poverty Targeting – Raw Data and Percentage Distribution by Per Capita Household Expenditure and Educational Attainment (Agip)**

| (N) | | Educational Attainment | | | Totals |
|---|---|---|---|---|---|
| | | Never schooled | FLSC/WASC | Tertiary | |
| Per capita Household Expenditure | 18,000-47,999(low) | 3 (14) | 19 (86) | 0 (0) | 22 (100) |
| | 48,000-99,999(average) | 5 (9) | 45 (77) | 8 (14) | 58 (100) |
| | 100,000 and above (high) | 5 (9) | 46 (85) | 3 (6) | 54 (100) |
| Totals | | 13 (10) | 110 (82) | 11 (8) | 134 (100) |

Calculated $x^2$: 5.160, Critical values of $x^2$: $x^2_{.05} = 9.488$, $x^2_{.10} = 7.779$

**Table 3 Evaluating Poverty Targeting – Raw Data and Percentage Distribution by Per Capita Household Expenditure and Type of Construction Material (Agip)**

| (N) | | Type and construction material | | Totals |
|---|---|---|---|---|
| | | Mud / wood and thatched/zinc roof | Concrete/ block and zinc roof | |
| Per capita Household Expenditure | 18,000-47,999 (low) | 4 (18) | 18 (82) | 22 (100) |
| | 48,000-99,999(average) | 13 (22) | 45 (78) | 58 (100) |
| | 100,000 and above (high) | 8 (15) | 46 (85) | 54 (100) |
| | Totals | 25 (19) | 109 (81) | 134 (100) |

Calculated $x^2$: 1.069, Critical values of $x^2$: $x^2_{.05} = 5.99147$, $x^2_{.10} = 4.60517$

**Table 4 Evaluating Poverty Targeting – Raw Data and Percentage Distribution by Per Capita Household Expenditure and Type of Dwelling (Agip)**

| (N) | | Type of Dwelling | | Totals |
|---|---|---|---|---|
| | | Owned | Rented | |
| Per capita Household Expenditure | 18,000-47,999 (low) | 16 (73) | 6 (27) | 22 (100) |
| | 48,000-99,999 (average) | 40 (69) | 18 (31) | 58 (100) |
| | 100,000 and above (high) | 42 (78) | 12 (22) | 54 (100) |
| Totals | | 98 (73) | 36 (27) | 134 (100) |

Calculated $x^2$: 1.107, Critical values of $x^2$: $x^2_{.05} = 5.991$, $x^2_{.10} = 4.605$

**Table 5 Evaluating Poverty Targeting – Raw Data and Percentage Distribution by Per Capita Household Expenditure and Sanitary Practice (Shell)**

| (N) | | Sanitary Practice | | Totals |
|---|---|---|---|---|
| | | Flush Toilet | Cover Pit/ Open Air | |
| Per capita Household Expenditure | 20,000-47,999 (low) | 2 (29) | 5 (71) | 7 (100) |
| | 48,000 and above (high) | 2 (13) | 13 (87) | 15 (100) |
| Totals | | 4 (18) | 18 (82) | 22 (100) |

Calculated $x^2$: 0.7444, Critical values of $x^2$: $x^2_{.05} = 3.841$, $x^2_{.10} = 2.706$

**Table 6 Evaluating Poverty Targeting – Raw Data and Percentage Distribution by Per Capita Household Expenditure and Sanitary Practice (Shell)**

| (N) | | Educational Attainment | | Totals |
|---|---|---|---|---|
| | | Never Schooled | FLSC/WASC | |
| Per capita Household Expenditure | 20,000-47,999 (low) | 0 (0) | 7 (100) | 7 (100) |
| | 48,000 and above (high) | 1 (7) | 14 (93) | 15 (100) |
| Totals | | 1 (5) | 21 ( 95) | 22 (100) |

Calculated $x^2$: 0.488, Critical values of $x^2$: $x^2_{.05} = 3.841$, $x^2_{.10} = 2.706$

**Table 7 Evaluating Poverty Targeting – Raw Data and Percentage Distribution by Per Capita Household Expenditure and Type of Construction Material (Shell)**

| (N) | | Type of Construction Material | | Totals |
|---|---|---|---|---|
| | | Mud/Wood and Thatched/Zinc Roof | Concrete/block and zinc roof | |
| Per capita Household Expenditure | 20,000-47,999 (low) | 2 (29) | 5 (71) | 7 (100) |
| | 48,000 and above (high) | 0 (0) | 15 (100) | 15 (100) |
| Totals | | 2 (9) | 20 (91) | 22 (100) |

Calculated $x^2$: 4.717, Critical values of $x^2$: $x^2_{.05} = 3.841$, $x^2_{.10} = 2.706$

**Table 8 Evaluating Poverty Targeting – Raw Data and Percentage Distribution by Per Capita Household Expenditure and Type of Dwelling (Shell)**

| (N) | | Type of Dwelling | | Totals |
|---|---|---|---|---|
| | | Owned | Rented | |
| Per capita Household Expenditure | 20,000-47,999 (low) | 6 (86) | 1 (14) | 7 (100) |
| | 48,000 and above (high) | 10 (67) | 5 (33) | 15 (100) |
| Totals | | 16 (73) | 6 (27) | 22 (100) |

Calculated $x^2$: 1.414, Critical values of $x^2$: $x^2_{.05} = 3.841$, $x^2_{.10} = 2.706$

Source: Survey Data 2006 and Authors' Calculation

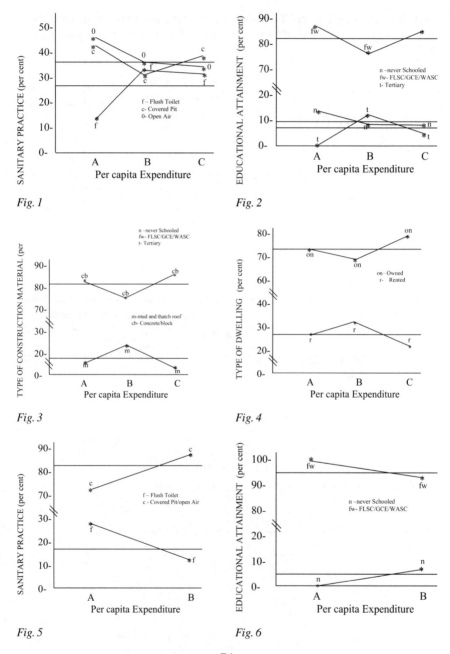

Fig. 1

Fig. 2

Fig. 3

Fig. 4

Fig. 5

Fig. 6

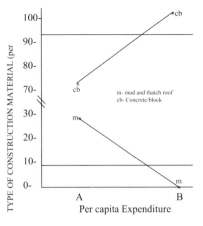

*Fig. 7*

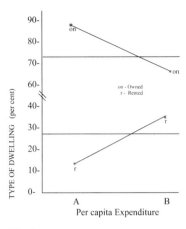

*Fig. 8*

## 5.6. References

Ajakaiye, O. and V. A. Adeyeye (2000). "The Nature of Poverty in Nigeria". Ibadan: Nigerian Institute of Social and Economic Research. Monograph Series. No. 13.

Akpakpan, E.B. (1991). *Economics beyond Demand and Supply*. Port Harcourt: New Generation Publishers

CASS – Centre for Advanced Social Science. (2003). "Poverty knowledge and Policy Process in Bayelsa State." Paper presented at the dissemination workshop organized by CASS in Collaboration with the Institute of Development Studies, University of Sussex, Brighton, U. K.

Eboreime, I.M. (2007). "Evaluation of Poverty Reduction Interventions of Selected Multinational Oil Firms in Nigeria's Niger Delta." An Unpublished PhD Dissertation. Imo State University, Owerri.

FINCA (1996). "Finca Annual Report and statement of Account". Finca International.

Grosh, M.E. and J. L. Baker (1995). "Proxy Means Test for Targeting Social Program: Simulations and Speculation." LSMS Working Papers. No. 18. Washington. D.C. World Bank.

Ikein, A, A. (1990). *The Impact of Oil in a Developing Country: The Case of Nigeria.* Ibadan: Evans Brothers Limited

Kumar, S. (1985). "Types of Impact Evaluation." In *Monitoring and Evaluation*. Agricultural Management Training for Africa (AMTA). EDI Washington, D.C.: World Bank

Leftwich, R. H. and A.M. Sharp (1980). *Economics of Social Issues* .Dallas: Business Publications Inc.

McClave, J.T. and P.G. Benson (1988). *Statistics for Business and Economics.* San Francisco: Dellen Publishing Company.

Nigerian Agip Oil Company (Undated). "Eni in Nigeria." Port Harcourt.

Nwosu, E.J. (2000). *The Challenge of Poverty in Africa.* Owerri: Skillmark Media Ltd.

Nyemutu Roberts, F.O. (1998). "Managing the Minorities and Development Problems in Nigeria Federalism: The OMPADEC Initiative." Monograph Series No. 11 Nigerian Institute of Social and Economic Research, Ibadan.

Obi, C. (1997). "Oil, Environmental Conflict and National Security in Nigeria:

Ramification of the Ecology-Security Nexus for Sub-Regional Peace". Arms Control and Disarmament and International Security Program. University of Illinois at Urbana-Champaign.

Olaide, S.O. and S.M. Essang (1975). "Aspects of Rural Poverty in Nigeria: Implication for Policy." In NES Conference Proceedings. "Poverty in Nigeria." Ibadan: Nigerian Economic Society.

Omene, G. E. (2003). "NDDC and Community Projects: Progress So Far." Paper Presented at the Centre for Petroleum Information. Petroleum Roundtable. Lagos. June 20.

Omotor, D.G. (2009). "The Impact of Oil Exploration on the Inhabitants of the Oil Producing Areas of Nigeria". *Journal of Food, Agriculture and Environment* (Forthcoming).

Prennushi G., Rubio G. and K. Subbarao (2002). "Monitoring and Evaluation." In World Bank: *A Source book for Poverty Reduction Strategies.* Vol. 1 Washington, D.C. World Bank.

Ross, M. (2003). "The National Resource Curse: How Wealth can Make You Poor." In Ian Bannon and Paul Collier ed. *Natural Resources and Violent Conflicts: Options and Actions.* Washington D. C.: World Bank.

Shell (2000). "A Sectoral Review of Women Development Programmes in the Niger Delta." SPDC. Port Harcourt.

Sincich, T. (1986). *Business Statistics by Example.* San Francisco: Dellen Publishing Company.

Thisday Editorial (2006, October 24). "Unacceptable Poverty Rate". Thisday. vol. 11 No. 4203. pp. 17

Todaro, M.P. (1979). *Economics for a Developing World.* London: Longman Group Limited.

United Nations (2001). *Nigeria: Common Country Assessment.* United Nations System in Nigeria. March.

Von Pischke J.D. (1991). *Finance at the Frontiers: Debt Capacity and the Role of Creditin the Private Economy.* Washington. D. C.: World Bank.

Wodon, Q. and S. Yitzhaki (2002)."Inequality and Social Welfare." In Jeni Clugman, ed., *A Source Book for Poverty Reduction Strategies.* **Washington D.C.: World Bank.**

Wonacott, P. and R. Wonacott (1979). *Economics* New York: McGraw – Hill Book Company.

World Bank (1983). *Focus on Poverty.* World Bank: Washington, D.C.

World Bank (2001). World Development Report. Washington, D.C.: Oxford University Press.

# 6. Governance failure, civil societies and the Niger Delta

Dr. Akpomuvire Mukoro

## 6.1. Introduction

The Niger Delta region of Nigeria is made up of nine (9) states. These comprise of Abia State, Akwa-Ibom State, Bayelsa State and Cross River State. Others are Delta State, Edo State, Imo State, Ondo State and Rivers state. These states collectively account for about 90% of Nigeria's foreign exchange earnings. This, no doubt, goes to show that Nigeria relies almost exclusively on crude oil and gas (Orubu, 2002).

Report has it that from the period when crude oil was first discovered up to 1995 (35 years after), the country made over US$350 billion (ANEEJ, 2004). This amount rose to US$694 billion in 2005 (ANEEJ, 2008), thus representing about 1.5% of the world's Gross Domestic Product for the year 2005. An account by the African Development Bank (ADB, 2002) has it that Nigeria is Africa's fourth largest economy after South Africa, Egypt and Algeria. The report has it that the aggregate real GDP and per capita real GDP growth rates are far below the 7.0% and 4.5% respectively, which is required to achieve a significant reduction in poverty and attain international development goals by 2015.

The Niger Delta region is the bedrock of Nigeria's crude oil production while Bayelsa, Delta and Rivers States account for 75% of oil production in the Niger Delta region. In spite of the enormous wealth that has been generated by the region to the Nigerian State, the region, according to Ekpebu (2002), presents a "perfect example of the paradox of excruciating poverty and misery in the midst of stupendous wealth, as the resources of the region have barely touched on their pervasive poverty." Resources misuse has transformed the region into a theatre of bloody confrontation, which is not good for national peace, investment and the country's image. Ownership of the crude resources in the region has since 1968, during the

79

Nigerian civil war, been transferred to the centre by the federal government rather than in the state or community where the product is located. It is an irony of life that a region that produces the wealth of the nation should remain poor and the people live in poverty. Nigeria has been described according to Igun (2008) as a "pathetic paradox: so rich and yet so poor; so endowed and yet so mismanaged; so much potential and yet so prodigal." Thus, structures of government in Nigeria have increasingly become a fiction in governance. As a highly centralised state, it is expensive to run, its operations are cumbersome, inflexible and subjected to being abused (Esman, 1991). The failure can also be traceable to a combination of uninhibited particularity such as corruption, incapacity to resolve social conflict peacefully, external pressure and intervention, rapid technological outclassing and economic incompetence. Available literature on governance shows that Nigerian government has not been doing well politically and economically. Because of this reason, emphasis should now be shifted to the growth of civil societies, public ownership of political institutions, mobilisation of talents and resources into constructive patterns and countervailing powers vis-a-vis national institutions. This position is re-enforced by the years of frustrating experience with highly centralised governance process here in Nigeria particularly as it affects the Niger Delta region.

The emergence of civil societies and informal groups has come about to fill the gap created by the numerous problems of governance which are corruption, inability to enforce the rule of law, human right abuses, lack of transparency and accountability, war and conflict, underdevelopment, hunger and starvation which are very prevalent in the Niger Delta region. This paper argues that there should be a jurisdictional integrity that recognises the political and legal competence of a unit of government to operate within a spatial and functional realm, where the citizens are enabled to give consent to and pass judgment on the exercise of authority by government. This implies the transfer of responsibilities and resources from the central government to local government and the development of network between local governments and local non-state actors like the civil societies, community organisations, non-governmental informal associations etc.

## 6.2.  Oil and the Niger Delta

An evaluation of the governance process of the Nigerian state shows it to be a predator state. There is generally lack of development in the country, particularly in the Niger Delta region in spite of the huge earnings that has come out from oil. Indeed, Nigeria's weak political institutions are roots of development failures in the Niger Delta. The Niger Delta is so relevant that it is now occupying a prominent place in international discussions. The place has been the engine room and the epicentre of Nigeria's economy. It is a major source of energy supply and, therefore, a viable asset to the world's industrial development.

A study carried out by Ekpebu (2008) states that recent analysis of poverty and Human Development Index (HDI) paints a very sordid picture of the Niger Delta as the area's HDI is as low as 0.564. This ranking, no doubt, places the Niger Delta region slightly above the country's overall HDI of 0.453. Comparatively, the region ranks lower than regions and nations with identical gas and oil resources such as Saudi Arabia (0.8000), United Arab Emirate (0.846), Kuwait (0.844), Libya (0.799), Venezuela (0.772) and Indonesia (0.67). The Highest ranking score for the HDI is 1.

Okoba (2008) presents a worrisome account of the terrible situation in Nigeria. He says that Nigeria is Sub-Saharan Africa's largest exporter of oil with a production figure of 2.3 million bpd. Nigeria's oil earnings, according to him, ranked only behind the world's oil giants – Saudi Arabia, Venezuela, Iran, and United Arab Emirates. Nigeria in the midst of this wealth records an overwhelming high level of poverty (with 70% living on less than US\$1 a day, 40% lack sanitation and safe water, 82% lacking access to regular power supply and 46% infant mortality rate.

An inventory of the gains of oil to the Nigerian economy definitely is a salutary exercise. A report by the Economic and Financial Crimes Commission (EFCC) in 2005 said that in 2003, 70% of the country's oil wealth was stolen (*Newswatch*, September 9, 2005). Scholars and commentators have not spared the nation in their condemnation. Nna and Eyenke (2004) paint Nigeria as a predatory contraption in which power is based not on the usual recognised broad public support, but on force and coercion, and the support of a narrow kleptomaniac, self seeking elite. It is their argument that state power faces few constraints. The elite maintain the exploitation of

the public and private resources for the gain of themselves through institutionalised practices by which oil revenues and crude oil are controlled and
stolen to grease the functioning of an intensive machinery of rent seeking
and political patronage. The *Punch* Newspaper captured it thus:

> The Niger Delta which is the centre of Nigeria's multibillion dollar oil industry is
> one of West Africa's most underdeveloped and violent regions. Though the region
> is the source of more than ninety percent of Nigeria's foreign earnings, the people
> are among the poorest in the country.

Without deluding oneself, it has to be made known that the people of the
Niger Delta have long been aware of the benefits of oil to their communities.
In 1966, for example, Isaac Adaka Boro from Kaiama community of the
present Rivers State carried out a rebellion by declaring the Niger Delta a
Republic. This anger was incensed by the palpable state of neglect, squalor
and criminal rate of appropriation of the people's wealth to the centre. This
was followed by Ken Saro-Wiwa's Movement for the Survival of the Ogoni
People (MOSOP) in 1990, the Supreme Egbesu Assembly (SEA), the Niger
Delta Volunteer Force (NDVF), the Movement for the Emancipation of the
Niger Delta (MEND), amongst several other groups and civil societies. All
these civil movements (definitely not militancy) came about as a result of
the fact that "the Nigerian state has subordinated everything including the
lives and the livelihood of the people as well as the environment" to criminal neglect and rape. The inability of the people of the Niger Delta to enjoy
their God given wealth for over four (4) decades now will continue to generate discontent, hate and the fight for self determination.

## 6.3. Whither the Gains/Curse of Oil

The discovery of crude oil has transformed many societies and nations economically, technologically, and socially. Nations that own the product have
particularly been the better for it. But the Nigerian situation is such that
the people in the Niger Delta where this commodity is found have become
not only third class citizens, but the underdogs of the nation. This irony
is captured graphically by the United Nations Development Programme
(UNDP) in 2006. This body said so much about the Niger Delta region
of Nigeria to the extent that that it said, ordinarily, the Niger Delta should

be a gigantic economic reservoir of national and international importance. Its rich endowment of oil and gas resources fed methodically into the international economic system in exchange for massive revenues that carry the promise of rapid socio-economic transformation within the delta itself. But, in reality, the Niger Delta is a region suffering from administrative neglect, crumbling social infrastructure and services, high unemployment, social deprivation, abject poverty, filth and squalor, and endemic conflict.

If one were to ask what gains or curse the discovery of oil has brought to the people of the Niger Delta, then one may have to hear Ogwugah (2006) out when he said: "... the oil which brought so much wealth to the nation and those in power, brought much poverty, disease, death, loss of livelihood etc to the people of the oil bearing areas."

Ibodje (2008) has so copiously put down the graphic image of this paradox. He opined that while the oil from the region remains the engine that drives the nation, the experiences on ground are troubling and ironic. The first thing that strikes the first time visitor to the region is the almost total lack of road in the area whose wealth is funding the gigantic infrastructural development in other parts of the country. Even more paradoxical is the fact that at the same time that the oil from the region is generating such enormous income to grease the wheel of governance in Nigeria, including unprecedented wealth in the hands of the governing elite from the majority ethnic groups in control of power, its production process has continued to cause serious environmental degradation, destruction of the local economy of the oil-bearing communities, and the pauperisation of the indigenes.

The discovery of oil brought about an entirely new vista into the governance process of the state. It gave birth to predatory thriving elite that stood policies on its head. The formulae for revenue allocation were suddenly upturned to give prominence to other criteria at the disfavour of derivation. Worst still, the infamous Land Use Decree of 1978 emasculated further whatever benefits were left with the people of the Niger Delta over their ownership of oil. According to Ibodje (2008):

A significant milestone in the move by the federal government to take over the ownership of the mineral resources in the Niger Delta and to increase the centralisation process was reached in 1978 when Olusegun Obasanjo enacted his infamous land use decree of that year. With the Niger Delta oil particularly in mind, the decree converted all land in the country, including the oil minerals obtained from them, into possession of the Federal Government.

The commentator went on to conclude that the 1979 constitution which was modified by Obasanjo gave the decree a constitutional backing. The central object of the decree was the enablement of the oil companies to continue to carry out their activities of degrading the environment without challenge from any community. A good portrayal of the extent of centralisation of the revenue that accrued from oil between 1960 and 2009 is captured in the table below.

**Table I: Oil revenue: Percentage to Producing States.**

| S/no | Years | Producing State % | Percentage Sharing of federal government |
|---|---|---|---|
| 1. | 1960-67 | 50 | 50 |
| 2. | 1967-69 | 50 | 50 |
| 3. | 1969-71 | 45 | 55 |
| 4. | 1971-75 | 45 plus offshore proceedings | 55 plus offshore proceedings |
| 5. | 1975-79 | 20 minus offshore proceedings | 80 plus offshore proceedings |
| 6. | 1979-81 | - | 100 |
| 7. | 1982-92 | 1.5 | 98.5 |
| 8. | 1992-99 | 3 | 97 |
| 9. | 1999-09 | 13 | 87 |

Source: See Ibodje in Oyovbaire (eds.). Governance and Politics in Nigeria: The IBB and OBJ years. pg 154

A cursory look at the table above shows that the Niger Delta region enjoyed 50% allocation of revenue between 1960 and 1969 from oil. After that period, what got to them from the federal allocation began a nose dive until between 1979 and 1981, when nothing got to the oil producing states. It was the upsurge of agitation from this neglect that brought about the marginal allocation of 1.5% between 1982 and 1992; 3% between 1992 and 1999 and 13% between 1999 and 2009. This marginal increase ends up in the pockets of the few collaborators in power, who are agents of the centre. The table states the obvious reason why the agitators and civil movements in the Niger Delta will continue to be on the increase. The arrogance of the state over the oppressed people of the Niger Delta has been on for too long when one considers Table 2 below, and sees the prominent position oil has occupied in terms of contributions to the income of the country.

**Table II: Contribution of oil to Government revenue in Nigeria**

| Year | Amount (million Naira) | | Amount (million Naira) | | Total |
| | Oil Revenue | Percentage | Oil Revenue | Percentage | |
| --- | --- | --- | --- | --- | --- |
| 1970 | 11111166.6 | 26.3 | 1111467.4 | 73.7 | 1111.6 |
| 1971 | 11111510.1 | 43.6 | 1111658.7 | 56.4 | 111168.8 |
| 1972 | 11111764.3 | 54.4 | 1111640.8 | 45.4 | 111405.1 |
| 1973 | 111016.0 | 59.9 | 1111679.3 | 40.1 | 116695.3 |
| 1974 | 113724.0 | 82.1 | 1111813.4 | 17.9 | 114537.4 |
| 1975 | 114271.5 | 77.5 | ·111243.2 | 22.5 | 115514.7 |
| 1976 | 115365.2 | 79.3 | 111400.0 | 20.7 | 116865.9 |
| 1977 | 116080.6 | 75.6 | 111961.8 | 24.4 | 118042.4 |
| 1978 | 114555.1 | 61.8 | 112815.2 | 38.2 | 117371.0 |
| 1979 | 118880.1 | 81.4 | 112031.6 | 18.6 | 110912.4 |
| 1980 | 112353.0 | 81.1 | 112880.2 | 18.9 | 115233.5 |
| 1981 | 118564.0 | 64.4 | 114726.1 | 35.6 | 113290.5 |
| 1982 | 117814.1 | 68.3 | 13618.8 | 31.7 | 11433.7 |
| 1983 | 1117253.0 | 691 | 113255.7 | 311 | 110508.7 |
| 1984 | 118269.0 | 73.5 | 112984.1 | 26.5 | 111253.3 |
| 1985 | 110923.1 | 72.6 | 114126.7 | 27.4 | 115050.4 |
| 1986 | 118107.0 | 64.4 | 114488.1 | 35.6 | 112595.8 |
| 1987 | 119027.0 | 751 | 116353.6 | 251 | 125380.6 |
| 1988 | 119831.1 | 71.9 | 117765.0 | 28.1 | 127596.7 |
| 1989 | 139130.1 | 72.6 | 114739.9 | 27.4 | 153870.4 |
| 1990 | 171887.0 | 73.3 | 126215.3 | 26.7 | 198102.4 |
| 1991 | 182666.0 | 81.9 | 118325.2 | 18.1 | 100991.6 |
| 1992 | 164078.0 | 86.2 | 126375.1 | 13.8 | 190453.2 |
| 1993 | 162102.0 | 84.1 | 130667.0 | 15.9 | 1192769.4 |
| 1994 | 160192.0 | 79.3 | 141718.4 | 20.7 | 201910.8 |
| 1995 | 324547.1 | 70.6 | 135439.1 | 29.4 | 459987.3 |

| 1996 | 369190.0  | 711  | 151000.0  | 291  | 520190.0  |
|------|-----------|------|-----------|------|-----------|
| 1997 | 1416811.1 | 71.5 | 1166000.0 | 28.5 | 1582811.1 |
| 1998 | 1289532.3 | 62.5 | 1174076.5 | 37.5 | 1463608.8 |
| 1999 | 1724422.5 | 76.3 | 1224765.4 | 23.7 | 1949187.9 |
| 2000 | 1591675.8 | 83.5 | 1314483.9 | 16.5 | 1906159.7 |
| 2001 | 1707562.8 | 76.5 | 1523970.1 | 23.5 | 2231532.9 |
| 2002 | 1230851.2 | 71.1 | 1500986.3 | 28.9 | 1731837.5 |
| 2003 | 2074280.6 | 80.5 | 1500815.3 | 19.5 | 2575895.9 |

Source: Ikelegbe, A. (2008), see his contribution to the International Conference on the Nigerian state, Oil industry and the Niger Delta. Pg. 3

The above information was derived from figures given by the Central Bank of Nigeria. If nothing else, at least it shows the quantum contribution that the Niger Delta region makes to the sustenance and survival of the Nigerian nation.

## 6.4. The twist and the turns

The Niger Delta region has over 606 oil fields for both offshore and on-shore exploration (ANEEJ, 2004). Each oil field is made up of several oil rigs and flow stations that terminate at a particular oilfield. In all of these, most of the oil communities have pipelines for crude and refined products crisscrossing their landscape. This is in addition to pipes conveying gas to their various destinations. The process of exploring for both crude oil and gas, and the distribution of the products themselves come with a lot of attendant problems which are of both immediate and long term negative consequences.

It is instructive to state here that despite the enormous wealth and abundant resources present in the Niger Delta region, its potentials for sustainable development remains unfulfilled. In addition to this, there is the problem of environmental degradation, youth restiveness, and outright war.

A quick rundown of some of the attendant oil exploration induced problems in the Niger Delta are summarised below:

a) Oil Spillage has become a major source of environmental degradation which results in the loss of lives and properties.

b) Pipeline vandalisation has become a recurring decimal in the Niger Delta. This practice in turn causes deforestation, pollution (water and air) and the loss of revenue.

c) Ethnic and inter-ethnic clashes and conflicts have become very prominent in the Niger Delta. This is particularly more rampant in Delta, Rivers and Bayelsa States (see Imobighe, Bassey and Asuni, 2002).

d) Hostage taking has taken a new twist in the struggle for the emancipation of the Niger Delta. This practice has so degenerated that major oil prospecting companies with expatriates in their employment have started re-locating from the Niger Delta, or closing shops to flee the country. Worst still, the hostage takers have turned their nefarious activities at both foreign oil workers and influential locals to demand for ransom.

e) State corruption has become a major problem in the sense that not only is the oil money stolen and misappropriated by leaders (politicians, military and technocrats), the leadership turn a blind eye to the atrocities of the multi-national oil companies against oil bearing communities, after collecting bribe and gratification.

f) Oil bunkering, a social evil and an instrument of sabotage, is carried out by the ruling elite and their local collaborators against the indigenes of the Niger Delta.

g) Evidence abound that virtually all leadership in Nigeria had been autocratic, dictatorial and predatory towards the Niger Delta. A clear picture of the state of decay, neglect ad attendant environmental problems in the Niger Delta is presented in Table III below. A close look at the table shows that four major distinct areas are identified as constituting problems with their attendant appendages. These major areas are:

1. Natural environment problems
2. Development related problems
3. Oil industry activities
4. Socio-economic problems.

These major problem areas have their minor appendages which are in themselves infectious to the land, the people and the communities of the Niger Delta. It can now be seen that oil induced problems in the Niger delta are numerous and hydra headed. But a major aspect of the problem which has been overlooked over the years is the problem that can be referred to as 'Deprivation and the cover-up Syndrome'.

h) Interestingly, the deprivation and the cover-up syndrome is applied by the multinational oil companies to deny the people of the Niger Delta employment into top management and decision making positions. Apart from marginally giving employment to indigenes of the Niger Delta as either contract staff or casual workers, multinational oil companies operating in the area prefer to employ foreigners and Nigerians from the major ethnic nationalities [tribes], such as the Hausa/Fulanis, the Yorubas and the Igbo's.

The other tribes have agreed to become wicked collaborators because they have everything to benefit. After all, it is neither their land nor their people subjected to the pain oil discovery in the Niger Delta has unleashed.

This arrogance the state has shown towards the people of the Niger Delta has been taken so far that while the non-Niger Deltans are free and can work anywhere in Nigeria including the Niger Delta region, people from this region are discriminated against outside of their enclave. The few people of the Niger Delta, who had the opportunity to work outside the region by virtue of their hard work, are constantly reminded that they are strangers in other parts of Nigeria. Such persons are not, therefore, allowed to live happily and aspire to the highest positions of their career even if it is a federal job.

## 6.5.  Civil society and governance in the Niger Delta

Wolpert (2001) asked a pertinent question while opening his discussion of civil society and governance in a regional and community context. He asked: "Why is civil society needed if governance is transparent, participatory, representative, responsive, accountable, and cost effective and just? . . . and why is governance needed if civil society itself has all these virtues?" Some admirers of civil society have defended its existence as the best training for citizenship and that it rescues government by reducing the demand on it.

An examination of the governance process in most African states has shown that centralised systems of governance have proved a total failure

**Table III: Ranking of major environmental Problems, social issues and priorities.**

| Problem Types | Problem subjects | Priority Ranking |
|---|---|---|
| Natural Environment | Coastal/River bank Erosion | Moderately High |
| | Flooding | Moderate |
| | Sedimentation/Silt | Low |
| | Substance | Low |
| | Exotic (water-hyacinth) | High |
| Development related | Land Degradation/Soil Fertility Loss | High |
| Oil Industry Activities | Agric. Decline/Shortened fallow | High |
| | Delta Forest loss (mangroves) | High |
| | Bio-diversity depletion | High |
| | Fisheries Decline | High |
| | Oil Spillage | Moderate |
| | Gas Flaring | Moderate |
| | Sewage and Waste Water | High |
| | Other chemical | Moderate |
| Socio-Economic Problems | Poverty | High |
| | Unemployment | High |
| | Community-oil company Conflict | High |
| | Intra Community Conflict | Moderate |
| | Conflict over land | High |
| | Inter-Community Conflict | High |
| | Inadequate compensation | High |
| | Displacement | Moderate |
| | Decay in social values | High |
| | Poor Transportation/high cost of fuel | |
| | Housing Pressure/Infrastructure | High |
| | Decay /Crime | High |

Source: Monday, D. Imobighe and Thomas O. Edafiagho (2002), the Petroleum Industry, the Economy and the Niger Delta Environment.

in most countries in Sub-Sahara Africa (Wunseh and Olowu, 1990). Kukah (2003) summarised the position of several scholars of governance in Africa thus: "... . what now pass for states in Africa are the product of arbitrary colonial arrangement." Kukah went on to sermonise that "the Nigerian state, was conceived, nurtured and sustained in violence." Knowing

89

that governance has failed in Nigeria, the compelling political challenge will now, therefore, be on how to mobilise collective power of civil societies to enable them shape and manage their own lives more democratically in a secure and sustainable way.

A developmental explanation for the niche of civil societies and governance and their linkages suggest that they evolve functionally within societies to address checks and balances and comparative advantage issues. Shortcomings, failure and excesses in one sector elicit corrective remedies in the other. Studies of the American Society suggest that civil societies are strong there because they have been involved in the evolution of their federalism structure and system of checks and balances between the branches and tiers of government; for example, to constrain centralised authority (Wolpert, 2001).

If we are to look at happenings around the world in the past four decades, it will be seen that civil societies in Eastern and Central Europe and Latin America played a major role in pushing for democratisation process while those societies were moving from authoritarian rule to multiparty democracy (Arato and Cohen, 1993). It is based on this understanding that a definition can be given to civil society as:

... civil society comprises the collectivity of those social organisations that enjoy autonomy from the state (i.e. are neither part of the state nor creatures of it) and have one important goals among others to influence the state on behalf of their members (Blair, 1997).

In this regard, civil societies surface in societies to fill the gaps created by the ineptitude of government. In Nigeria, for example, this gap arises from the over centralisation of governance, economic crises, poverty and impoverishment, decline in basic social services, corruption, absence of the rule of law, and insecurity etc. The promotion of transparency and good governance has started catching the attention of many stakeholders, especially concerning the Niger Delta. There has been unprecedented number of summits, conferences, stakeholders' meetings, policy initiatives and bills introduced into state legislatures on transparency, accountability, revenue and fiscal management and development policies. All these initiative and pronouncement may end up as it has always been (rudderless), if cognisance is not paid to the activities of civil societies. Policy reform alone will not be enough. All stakeholder groups need to work together with a common vision and purpose.

An organised civil society, according to Diamond (1995), should possess the following attributes:

– An organised civil society serves as a check against the excesses of government, human rights violations, abuse of the rule of law, monitoring of the application of constitutional provisions.
– Increases the participation and the skills of all the various segments of society, and it instils a sense of tolerance, thrift, hard-work, moderation, compromise among the various competing parties in the society.
– It serves as an alternative to political parties and can offer a refuge for those who are shut out from their rights due to non-membership of given political parties.
– It serves to enhance the bargaining power of interest groups and provide inclusive mechanism for them.
– It has a role in mitigating the excesses of fundamentalist, extremist and Maximalist who tend to have a very narrow view of life in the context of either/or. It thus also provides other alternative for negotiation within a multi-faceted society.
– It can serve as recruiting ground for, and the training of prospective member of the political or economic class to enhance the quality of participants in government. In effect, it is a leadership recruitment field.

Several civil societies have sprung up in the Niger Delta region of Nigeria. Virtually all the oil producing communities have women forming one kind of association or the other. These women groups have been very successful at staging protests against the government. The women wing of MOSOP, for example, locked their market stalls, abandoned their farms, stopped their children from going to school and staged a peaceful protest with the youths and the men. This protest coincided with the inauguration of UN international year of the world's indigenous people in Ogoni land. The Niger Delta women's role in the development of the region reached a crescendo on 8 July 2002 when 2000 women from Ugborode and Ugboegungun in Warri South Local Government in Delta State laid siege at the Chevron Escravos Tank Farm, a major crude oil storage and export facility owned and operated by the Chevron/NNPC Joint Venture. The women refused entry and exit of anybody from the facility, thereby bringing the operations of the multi-national company to a standstill. This account by Akpotor and Azelama (2003) went on to tell us that a combined group of Itsekiri, Ilaje and Ijaw women numbering about three thousand seized the Warri operational Headquarters of Shell and Chevron-Texaco on 8 August 2002. The women did what they did because they have lost faith in the system and, so, decided to do it their way.

Following the revelation that Governor Alamieyeseigha of Bayelsa State is involved in reckless financial management, the Bayelsa Women Forum made a public advertorial that he should not be returned to Government House. This strategy yielded immense result as, within a short while, the governor was removed from office. Apart from associations like MOSOP, groups like Ijaw Youths Council (IYC), Chikoko Movement (CM), and Movement for the Survival of the Ijaw Ethnic Nationality in the Niger Delta (MOSIEND), Movement for the Restoration of Ogbia (MORETO), Supreme Egbesu Assembly (SEA), Niger Delta Volunteers Force (NDVF) and Movement for the Emancipation of the Niger Delta (MEND) also exist. The above mentioned associations have been more involved with civil and awareness movement/mobilisation. Although some of their activities have been rather vicious, the use of maximum force by these groups has been necessitated in most cases by the nonchalant attitude of the state.

In all, the categories of civil societies existing in the Niger Delta region can be broken down into Town/Village Unions and Community Development Association (CDA's), which are present in virtually all communities in the region. Others are trade and professional guilds, women groups, religious organisations, social clubs, kindred, age-grades, thrift and credit unions etc. These mentioned bodies and associations have been known to be involved with the construction of roads and bridges, building of schools and health facilities, management of markets, construction of police stations, court houses, community banks, revenue generation and labour mobilisation for community projects and for mutual aid and welfare (Olowu and Erero, 1997). Apart from the above mentioned roles which civil societies play, many of them are now known to arrange for their internal security by organising vigilante groups for the purpose of maintenance of law and order, peace- keeping, provision of security, and conflict resolution. The youths and middle aged men are found more in these groups.

## 6.6.  Linkages between civil societies and governance in the Niger Delta

Efforts to understand civil society and governance and their linkages in the Niger Delta are likely to be enhanced considerably through focused attention on scale and diversity issues that affect immediate communities and their surroundings in the Niger Delta. For one, civil societies that focus on the community have to be involved with civil engagement because they are the vehicle for enhancing the quality and variety of life in ways that are not in the arena of government. These concern civil societies that are more social, and that pursue more of welfare issue. Engagements provide experience, skills and networks that might even yield cohesiveness and better citizenship in a participatory democracy. Groups in this category advance the social good of their members and their niche is co-operative rather than competitive. But the more common civil societies found in the Niger Delta region pursue issues that will help them to preserve their local autonomy, liberty, home rule and independence by countering, providing and compensating for failures in centralised government systems. Focusing on issues that affect their surrounding makes civil societies to operate as instruments in parallel positions with government structures. In essence, they exist to strengthen the participation of individuals and groups in creating a good life and a better future for the society. Civil societies have tasks to perform in responding to threats of encroachment or negligence of government by guiding and encouraging government and the political process to become more responsive to the citizenry. In this wise, civil societies do what government cannot do well and, thus, encourage government to be effective in functions that concern the welfare and liberty of the citizens. Also, civil societies can provide protection, not only from intrusive or neglectful government, but also from corporate power (for example, safeguard against discrimination and hazardous practices by private firms and multi-national organisations).

In other respect, the linkages that exist between civil society and government can be recognised through their formal and informal structures. Although formal linkages may not be too prominent, yet they serve purposes of ratification and consultation over appointment into government portfolios. They serve a better purpose in this wise since they can truly represent the interests of their communities and interest groups more than those the government has imposed on the people. Informal links would include collaboration between law enforcement agents and the people through their vigilante groups. This will help to fight crime and ensure peace. In another respect, this move gives credence to the need for community policing. Virtually all the communities in Ughelli North Local government of Delta State are paraded by the Bakassi vigilante group, and it can be seen that the rate of crime has come down drastically.

One other area of linkage that we can identify is the existence of civil societies in the rural communities, which are also being represented in urban centres. In this way, societies in rural communities resident in urban areas participate in the governance of their communities and, also, protect the interest of the community members that are resident in the urban centres. In some urban communities, according to Olowu and Erero (1997), "traditional rulers have seen the wisdom of appointing chiefs from migrant communities to oversee the affairs of such migrants." At such conditions, there is no way peace will not prevail amongst the community of men.

## 6.7. Conclusion and recommendations

There are different varieties of civil societies currently in the Niger Delta region. They deal with different aspects and areas of human endeavours, which make them rich in their diversity. This diversity is reflected in the range of activities used to describe their work: welfare, development, environmental, indigenous, gender, human rights, mobilization, advocacy, income generating, job creation, and so forth (Mogella, 1999). As the government's capacity to meet the needs of the citizens has become increasingly low and poor, civil societies now have to be involved in providing social services, employment generation, environmental concerns, commerce, policy formulation, mobilisation and advocacy, poverty alleviation and general security.

It has to be made clear that civil societies play important and unique roles in strengthening governance. Because of the unending strife in the Niger Delta region, attention has to be shifted to consider the fact that there are new emerging relations between state and civil societies through policy dialogue. Members of civil societies should be invited to give their views or opinions on the several contentious issues to enable government have a balanced judgment over issues. The recent amnesty granted the Niger Delta militants by the federal government late in the month of June 2009 cannot work. Technically speaking, who should be granting amnesty to whom? Should it be the aggressor or the aggrieved? The militants kidnapping people to ask for ransom or monetary reward qualify to be granted amnesty. But those legitimate freedom fighters and civil society movement who are in the struggle to stop the arrogance of the Nation over their property, resources, environment and land, definitely have to be engaged in dialogue. The federal government does not own the revenues in each community of the nation. The assignment of the responsibility to collect revenues should not be taken as making the collecting agents the exclusive owner of such resources. In Canada, for example, the central government has no access to national resources. They are collected by the provinces (Vincent Ola, 2002).

A major concern that has to be taken to heart is that civil societies enjoy legitimacy amongst their members. They also have stable and enduring acceptance amongst their members. Checks and balances exist in their operations and they can easily resolve conflicts amongst themselves and other groups. This is the caveat that government should embrace and explore while handling issues of dispute in the Niger Delta. Fundamentally, traditional values and norms which emphasise good governance can be harnessed and promoted by the elite, who are increasingly assuming position of responsibility in government and industry. We must not forget that these groups provide opportunity for building a better nation by adapting, among others, local efforts at decentralisation, federal arrangement and arrangements that enable people from different parts of Nigeria to live together in a community while synthesising urban and rural resources and elements for reforming formal agencies of government for good governance in the Niger Delta region.

A final conclusion that will be made in this paper is that government must recognise the consolidated strengths of civil societies, especially non-governmental organisations (NGOs). No amount of development, democracy and governance can be attained without building on the valued social structures which exist in civil societies and with which the people identify.

# 6.8. References

Africa Development bank (ADB) Report 2002.

Africa Network for Environment and Economic Development (ANEEJ), 2004.

Akpotor, A. S. and Azelama, J. U. (2003) *"Peace – violent women activities and Critical Development in the Niger Delta"* In Iyoha, F. E., Ojo, S. O. J. and Oviasuyi, P. O (ed). Women, Youth Restiveness and development in the Niger Delta. Ekpoma Institute for Governance and development. A. A. U.

ANEEJ (2008).

Arato, A. and Cohen, J. (1993) Civil Society. Cambridge. MIT Press.

Blair, H. (1997), *"Donors, Democratization and civil Society: Relating Theory and Practice"* in Hulme, D. and Edwards, M (eds) NGO's, State and Donors: Too Close for Comfort. London McMillian Press Limited.

Diamond, L. (1995) *Rethinking Civil Society* (Crossroads, USIS newsletter) Lagos February 1995.

Ekpebu, L. (2008)*"The State, Oil Companies and the Niger Delta"* in the Nigerian State, Oil Industry and the Niger Delta. Port Harcourt: Harey Publication Company.

Esman, M. (1991), *Management Dimensions of Development: Perspectives and Strategies*. Kumarien Press: West Hartford, Lonn.

Ibodje, S. W. E. (2008) *"Oil and the Niger Delta"* in Sam Oyovbaire (ed) Governance and Politics in Nigeria: The IBB and OBJ Years. Ibadan, Spectrum Books Limited.

Igun, U. A. (2008), *"Power, Distributive System and the Niger Delta Crisis"* in Nigerian Sociological Review, Vol. 3. No. 1 and 2.

Ikeleghe, A. (2008) *"Integrating a Crisis of Corporate Governance and the Interface with Conflict: The Case of Multinational oil Companies and the Conflict in the Niger Delta'* in International Conference on the Nigerian State, Oil Industry and the Niger Delta, Port Harcourt: Harey Publications company.

Imobighe, D. M. and Edafiagho T. O. (2002) *"Basic Infrastructure and Poverty Alleviation: The Case of Oil Producing States in the Niger Delta"* in Orubu *et al* The Petroleum Industry, The Economy and The Niger Delta Environment. Abraka, Delta State University.

Imobighe, T. A., Bassey, C. O. and Asuni, J. B. (2002) Conflict and Instability in the Niger Delta: The Warri Case. Ibadan Spectrum Books Limited.

Also, see Otite Onigu and Albert Olawale Isaac (Ed: 2004), Community conflicts in Nigeria: Management, Resolution and Transformation. Ibadan, Spectrum books Limited.

Kukah, M. H. (2003), Democracy and Civil Society in Nigeria. Ibadan, Spectrum Books Limited.

Mogella, C. (1999) *The State and Civil Society relations in Tanzania*: *The case of the National MGD's Policy*. Department of Political Science and Administration, University of Dar es Salaam. East Africa Comparative Research Project on civil Society and Governance.

Nna, N. K. and Eyenke, C. (2004) *"Oil Spillage, Sabotage and the Politics of Exclusion in the Niger Delta"* in V. T. Jike (ed) Social Problem, theoretical Paradigm in Contemporary Sociology. Lagos NISS Publication.

Okoba, B (2008) *"Petrodollar, the Nigerian State and the Crisis of Development in the Niger Delta Region: Trends, Challenges and the Way Forward"* in the Nigerian State, Oil INDUSTRY and the Niger Delta. Port Harcourt: Harey Publication Company.

Olowu, D. and Eroro, J. (1997) Indigenous Governance System in Nigeria. Ile-Ife, Obafemi Awolowo University L.I.S.D.P.

Orubu, C. O. (2002) *"Introduction"* in Orubu C. O., Ogisi D. O. and Okoh R. D. (Ed) The Petroleum Industry, the Economy and the Niger Delta Environment. Delta State University, Department of Economics.

Ogwugah, L. (2000), *"The Political Economy of resistance in the Niger Delta"*, Environmental Rights Action. Benin City.

Punch Newspaper (2003), editorial of November 12.

UNDP (2006), Niger Delta Human Development Report. U.N House Abuja.

Vincent, O. (2002) *"Fiscal federalism: The Nigerian Experience"* in The Nigerian Tribune. Tuesday, January 29th.

Wolpart, J. (2001),*Civil Society and governance in regional and community Context*.' Princeton, Woodrow Wilson School, Princeton University, New Jersey.

Wunsch, J. And Olowu, D. (Eds) (1990) The Failure of centralized State Institutions and Self – Governance in Africa. Boulder: Westview Press.

# 7. Niger Delta Technical Committee (NDTC) and the Niger Delta Question

J. Shola Omotola

## 7.1. Introduction

The paper primarily sets out to undertake a critical analysis of the problems and prospects of the NDTC vis-à-vis the Niger Delta question. The NDTC was inaugurated on 8 September 2008 by the Yar 'Adua's administration to "collate, review and distil" various reports, suggestions and recommendations from previous reports on the Niger Delta, including the Willinks Commission Report of 1958 in order to chart alternative way forward in redressing the Niger Delta question. On the surface, this seems an overtly timely and appropriate objective, given that the region is awash with a plethora of such committees in the past with little or no action on the reports of such committees. Moreover, the Niger Delta question, defined largely in terms of oil and environmental politics and insecurity (Omotola, 2006; 2007; 2009a), has always been a campaign issue during elections since 1999 when Nigeria returned to the path of democracy. For example, finding a lasting solution to the Niger Delta question was one of the main campaign issues of Obasanjo in 1999, which eventually informed the subsequent establishment of the Niger Delta Development Commission (NDDC) (Omotola, 2007). President Umar Musa Yar'Adua did same. Little wonder that after his inauguration, Yar'Adua made the Niger Delta question one of the seven point agenda of his administration (Omotola, 2009c).

Recent events in the region have made it important to reassess recent initiatives at redressing the Niger Delta question. Specifically, the May 2009 protracted 'war' between the Joint Military Task Force (JTF), deployed to the region for security reasons, and the militant movements represents the toughest. In the ensuing battle, there has been indiscriminate bombardment, sacking of communities, wanton destruction of properties, killing of innocent civilians, and violation of women and children's rights. These were in addition to extensive displacement of people and rising refugee population. These developments signify one thing: the failure of recent state interventions in the region, including the NDTC. While it may be too early to draw a definite conclusion on the NDTC, the fact that the federal government has not issued a white paper on the report, which was submitted to it on 28 November 2008, gives the impression of a hidden agenda.

This paper interrogates the theoretical underpinnings of the NDTC, assesses its rationales, probes its composition, and evaluates its terms of reference and reports. The paper argues that given the lessons of recent political history of the country, replete with such numerous committees without positive change, the NDTC has limited possibilities of contributing to the effective resolution of the Niger Delta question. Apart from notable contradictions in the framework of the NDTC, as this paper will reflect, the announcement by the federal government of the establishment of a separate federal ministry for the Niger Delta, barely a week after the inauguration of the committee, suggests the insincerity of the government. It suggests that the composition of the committee in the first place may be an ambush for strong oppositional voices in the region. The eventual emergence of Ledum Mitee, the president of the Movement for the Survival of the Ogoni People (MOSOP), as the chairman of the committee, after the unsuccessful attempt by the government to impose one, attests to this. By implication, the political will to execute the report of the committee may be missing *ab initio*.

In the first section, the paper sketches issues in the Niger Delta question. The second gives a brief review of previous committees and their reports on the Niger Delta, what is referred to in this study as reports unlimited without action and positive change. The next section critically analyses the NDTC, showing its ups and downs vis-à-vis the Niger Delta question. The last section recapitulates the main position of the paper, before concluding with a brief sketch of the challenges ahead.

## 7.2. The Niger Delta question

The Niger Delta question has for years become a critical element of the national question in Nigeria, which is a combination of all crucial issues of national significance that can impact, for good or for ill and depending on their management, on the process of nation-building, sustainable democracy and development. These include the question of true federalism, revenue allocation, resource control, group autonomy, secularism and religious balancing and so on. Out of these, the Niger Delta question stands out for its security, environmental, health and developmental implications (Naanen, 1995, 2001).

The Niger Delta is the heartbeat of the Nigerian national political economy. It is Nigeria's oil-rich enclave located in the riverrine areas of the south-south, and it covers an area of about 70,000 kilometres$^2$, half of which is wetland and has been a contentious site of oil and environmental politics since the commencement of oil production in the region. The area is inhabited by notable ethnic minorities, which the Willink Commission Report estimated to have seventeen (17) major languages and some 300 of lesser importance in the region. Some of the major ethnic groups include the Ijaw, Urhobo, Ogoni, Itsekiri, Efik, Ibibio and a host of others.

The Niger Delta harbours Nigeria's vast oil and gas deposit to the tune of 33 billion barrels and 160 trillion cu. ft, respectively. From oil alone, Nigeria generated about US$300 billion between 1970 and 2000, amounting to 96% of the country's foreign earnings (Okonjo-Iweala, Soludo and Murktah, 2003). In 2006, the Nigerian government estimated it was earning about $36 billion each year from the extensive petroleum industry (Osuaka, 2007). Other estimates, however, put current annual earnings at over $45 billion (Human Rights Watch, 2007:16). These oil revenues accrue to the federation account from where it is shared among the three tiers of government – federal, state and local.

Despite the huge petro-earnings over the years, Nigeria remains one of the poorest countries in the world. The level of penury seems worse in the Niger Delta due to oil exploitation and attendant oil and environmental politics. Years of oil activities have resulted in excruciating pollution of the environment through incessant oil spills and gas flaring. This has had serious implications on the survival of the people, denying them of their sources of living, most notably fishing and farming. A government source documents 6, 817 spills, practically, one a day for 25 years. But analysts suspect the real number may be ten times higher (O'Neil, 2007: 102). This is a well-found suspicion. In an astonishing revelation, the United Nations

J. Shola Omotola

Development Programme (UNDP) in its Niger Delta Human Development Report, 2006, reported a total of 1,100,000 barrels oil spills in the Niger Delta between 1979 and 2005 (UNDP, 2006: 184; quoted in Opukri and Ibaba, 2008:181). The breakdown is as follows:

**Table 1: Summary of some oil spills in the Niger Delta, 1979-2005**

| Episode | Year | State | Qty spilt in Barrels |
|---|---|---|---|
| Forcados terminal oil spills | 1979 | Delta | 570,000 |
| Funiwa No.5 well blow out | 1980 | Rivers | 400,000 |
| Oyekama oil spillage | 1980 | Rivers | 10,000 |
| System 2c Warri-Kaduna Pipeline rupture at Abudu | 1982 | Edo | 18,000 |
| Sohika oil spill | 1983 | Rivers | 10,000 |
| Idoho oil spill | 1983 | Akwa-Ibom | 40,000 |
| Jones Creek oil spill | 1998 | Delta | 21,000 |
| Jesse oil spill | 1998 | Delta | 10,000 |
| Etiama oil spill | 2000 | Bayelsa | 11,000 |
| Ughelli oil spill | 2005 | Delta | 10,000 |
| | | TOTAL | 1,100,000 |

Source: UNDP, 2006; Opukri and Ibaba, 2008:181.

Gas flaring has also been a constant source of worry in the Niger Delta, with devastating effects on the environment especially the degradation of the air. In 1991 when Nigeria's gross gas production was 31,500,000 standard cubic feet (scf), about 24,240,000cf of it were flared. This amounts to about 76 per cent of gross production of gas. It is unnecessarily too high in comparative terms. For instance, it was 0.6, 0.0, 4.3, 1.5, 5.0, 21.0, 20.0 and 19.0% for the USA, Holland, Britain, former USSR, Mexico, Libya, Saudi Arabia, and Algeria during the same period respectively (Opukri and Ibaba, 2008:181; Roberts, 2000: 33). By 1995, 76.79% of gross gas production in Nigeria was flared into the air. As a result, about 30 to 35 million tons of carbon dioxide and an estimated 12 million tons/year of methane, which is very dangerous to the environment, are emitted into the atmosphere. This has resulted in negative implications for the environment most notably increasing 'ambient air degradation' and attendant health hazards in the oil-producing areas (Roberts, 2000: 34).

102

The cumulative effects of oil spills and gas flaring have been devastating. Not only do they destroy environmental resources, damaging farmlands, rivers and their resources, but also deny the people of their livelihood. This partly explains the high rate of unemployment and rising poverty in the Niger Delta. Some of the health implications of the gaseous pollutants released into the atmosphere such as carbon dioxide, chlorine, nitrogen oxides, sulphur oxides, acid aerosol and beryllium include headaches, heart problems, irritation, oedema, dizziness and gene or neuron problems, depending on the pollutants (Kaladumo, 1996: 35).

To make matters worse, what the Niger Delta lost to oil production and attendant environmental dislocations, they have not been able to gain through power politics. Power politics is everywhere central to the allocation of resources, notably revenue allocation, distribution of government patronages and protection of minority rights, among others. Unfortunately, the Niger Delta has, until very recently, possibly for the twist and turns of their agitations and protests, has always been on the lower rung of power politics in Nigeria. Consequently, the region has enjoyed limited patronage from the federal government in terms of developmental projects and proactive environmental security plans and policies. In the thick of deepening developmental woes and environmental recession, the region began to agitate forcefully for true federation where greater latitude of autonomy would be conferred on the federating units, including the power of control over 'their' resources. Their agitations also include demand for more equitable revenue allocation formulae, where greater weight would be assigned to derivation to the tune of at least 25% subject to an annual upward review after five years (Saliu and Omotola, 2008).

These and related issues formed the benchmark of the Niger Delta's demands on the state at the 2005 National Political Reform Conference (NPRC). At the NPRC, they had forcefully made these points, arguing that if the oil were to be in the South West or the North, they would not have waited till 2005 to redress associated contradictions. Understandably, the Niger Delta people attributed their helplessness to their lack of political power, given their poor location in the power matrix of the country. Interestingly, the NPRC largely consented to the validity of these submissions. Professor John A. Ayoade, a delegate to the NPRC, shed more illuminating lights on the Niger Delta question at the NPRC. He reveals the submissions

103

of delegates from the Niger Delta and the acquiescence of the NPRC that the Niger Delta question would have been long resolved if they had political power. He, therefore, blamed the disjunction between the locations of political power and natural resources (oil) for the Niger Delta crisis (Ayoade, 2008).

Given the controversy that trailed the Niger Delta question at the NPRC, the inability to reach a consensus on the matter, it forcing the NPRC into about three weeks of recess and its eventual winding up unceremoniously, the importance of the Niger Delta question can no longer be in doubt. The squandering of the opportunity offered by the NPRC represents a critical element to the understanding of rising violence in the region.


## 7.3. Reports unlimited without action: from Henry Willinks Commission to the NDTC

It is correct to say that the attempt to manage the Niger Delta question has been largely predicated upon the ideology of establishing one form of committee or the other. This approach can be traced to the twilight of the colonial government in Nigeria. As the colonial government began a gradual process to wind up, efforts were made to address some vexed national issues including the minority question. In a recent but deeply incisive piece, Agbo (2009:20) identified at least fourteen (14) of such committees before the NDTC that were either directly or indirectly related to the Niger Delta. The first was the Henry Willinks Commission of 1958, which was set up essentially to look into the genuineness or otherwise of the fear of domination expressed by the minorities and their agitation for the creation of a separate state of their own, different from the majority-dominated states. The commission was also tasked with the responsibility of suggesting ways of allaying such fears. Although the commission found evidence in support of the authenticity of the fear of domination expresses by the ethnic minorities, it however, failed to accede to their demand for a separate state. Instead, the commission recommended the constitutional entrenchment of a bill of rights and the creation of s special commission to handle the problem of the region (Omotola, 2009; Osaghae, 1986; 1991; 1995; 1998). This led to the proclamation of the Niger Delta as a special area on 26 August 1959 and the setting up of the Niger Delta Development Board (NDDB).

The contradictions of the Willinks Commission, particularly its failure to grant the agitations of the ethnic minorities, despite establishing the validity of the claims, have been identified as one of the fundamental bases of the fluctuating fortunes of Nigerian federalism (Akinyele, 1996; Naanen, 1995).

Ever since, several other committees on the Niger Delta have come up. These included the Justice Alfa Belgore Judicial Committee of 1992. The committee was set up to look into the crisis of petroleum shortage in Nigeria. The committee recommended, among others, the establishment of a 30-year development plan for the Niger Delta, a recommendation that did not see the light of the day. Then came the Don Etiebet Report of 1994; the Vision 2020 Report of 1996; the United Nations Special Rapporteur on human Rights Situation in Nigeria of 1997; and Popoola Report of 1998, all of which were wholly or substantially devoted to the Niger Delta question, detailing the plight of the region and suggesting measures to address them (Agbo, 2009).

The General Alexander Ogomudia's Special Security Committee Report on Oil Producing Areas of 2002 was unique for the comprehensiveness of its mandates and recommendations (Ukoha, 2008; Adaka Boro Centre, 2008). The Committee was set up by the federal government in 2001 to identify lapses in the protection of oil installations including causes and sources of facility vandalisation and sabotage and recommend appropriate measures to enhance oil installation security; appraise the negative impact of youth and community agitations and recommend measures to reduce youth restiveness, communal agitations, and other incidents of sabotage of pipelines in oil communities. Other terms of reference of the Committee were to identify major interests and beneficiaries behind breaches of normal operations in the oil industry; investigate cases of illegal bunkering/vandalisation of pipelines resulting in loss of crude oil and siphoning of refined petroleum products, identify those behind the illegal acts and ensure their prompt arrest and prosecution; appraise the role of oil companies and other stakeholders, in terms of community relations and control of criminal acts, in the oil producing areas; assess long-term measures and strategies for protection and safety of Nigeria's vital oil resources, on-shore and off-shore, including strategies for improving inter-governmental cooperation and recommend appropriate measures to enhance their effectiveness, and achieve lasting peace and economic development in the area; coordinate inter-governmental (federal, state and local government) and inter-service operations to restore sanity to the Niger Delta area and reduce the frequency of criminal acts of lawlessness by individuals and groups. The committee also has responsibility to work out in detail, short, medium and long term security measures to adequately protect oil and gas installations from vandalisation, sabotage, terrorism and all forms of enemy activity; and make any other recommendations that may assist in the achievement of sustainable peace and development in the area.

The recommendations of the committee covered short, medium and long terms. For the short term, the committee recommended that there should be an upward review of the minimum 13% derivation to not less than 50%; government should enact laws that would make it mandatory for the creation of manufacturing companies to produce local content for oil producing companies; communities should be made to diversify into agricultural production unique to their environment; civic centres should be created for development of sports and extracurricular activities to engage youths during idle periods; mobilisation of youths to form labour vanguard for community developments; indigenes of oil producing communities must be trained for employment in the oil companies; immediate commencement of trans-coastal highway from Ondo State to Cross River State; provision of marine/Coastal mass transit transportation system; dredging of Eastern Obolo

(Akwa Ibom State), Ayetoro waterway and establishment of marine transportation and establishment of police stations in oil producing communities.

The medium term measures proposed by the Committee included sand filling of swamps to create new towns; erosion control; control of ocean surge of coastal area; provision of infrastructure such as electricity, water, roads etc; and that the National Boundary Commission should embark upon and complete boundary demarcation to avoid conflicts. At the level of long term, the Committee recommended all obnoxious laws, including the Land Use Act, Petroleum Act, Gas Re-injection Act and other laws which dispossess oil producing areas of their land, be repealed. It also recommended the speedy industrialisation of the area (Ukoha, 2008; Adaka Boro Centre, 2008).

The 2005 National Political Reform Conference (NPRC) conveyed to address the national question in Nigeria represented another major committee where the Niger Delta question ranked high (Saliu and Omotola, 2008; Omotola, 2006). Indeed, the topicality of the Niger Delta question to Nigeria's national question came to the fore when the controversies surrounding the Niger Delta issue forced the conference into an untimely and uncelebrated end.

The foregoing reveals that the problem of the Niger Delta is not that of committees and reports on what are to be done. Already, there are too many of such reports. The problem basically has to do with the non-implementation, or at best haphazard implementation of these reports depending on the discretion of the government of the day. The establishment of these committees may, therefore, be nothing more than part of the grand designs of the government to present itself as always interested in, and also doing something about the Niger Delta question. This way, the government seeks not only to buy popular legitimacy, but to discredit and weaken popular agitations and dissents in the region, also. It also served to provide some form of legitimisation for official excesses in the region, as the recent military escapade would suggest (Omotola, 2009). It is on this note that the setting up of another committee in the mode of the NDTC raises fundamental questions than answers, to which the next section of the paper addresses.

## 7.4. The Niger Delta Technical Committee (NDTC)

The NDTC was set up on 8 September 2008 with the primary responsibility to 'collate, review and distil the various reports, suggestions and recommendations on the Niger Delta from Sir Henry Willinks Commission Report on the fears of the minorities (1958) to General Alexander Ogomudia's Special Security Committee Report on Oil Producing Areas (2002) and on to the Report of the National Political Reform Conference (2005)' (Goodluck, 2008: 3). Its other terms of reference were to appraise the summary recommendations and present detailed short, medium and long-term suggestions, and make and present to the federal government any other recommendations that will help it achieve sustainable development, peace and human and environmental security in the Delta region.

The specific mention of three existing reports may suggest that in official circles, those three reports were the most relevant to the government in dealing with the tasks at hand. But it may also be an indictment on the government, suggesting that the government itself does not have an up-to-date file on the Niger Delta from where it could generate full list of previous reports on the Niger Delta. It, therefore, tactically shifted the task of searching for these reports on the NDTC. As Goodluck (2008:3) charged the NDTC at its inauguration: 'wherever a report on the Niger Delta exists and you can reach, I urge you to have them ferreted out; examined as thoroughly as you can and make suggestions for Government's necessary and urgent action.' The Vice President assured the committee, on behalf of the Government though, that the recommendations of the committee would not be treated with levity.

On paper, the establishment of the NDTC seems a timely and an appropriate intervention in the Niger Delta question, given the prevailing reality at the time. First, the level of protests and criminality in the region had reached an alarming proportion. It was such that in 2008 alone, 92 attacks on the oil industry were recorded. International Crisis Group estimated these to be 'about one third above the previous year' (ICG Policy Briefing, 2009:2). As a result, crude oil exports fell to 1.6 million barrels per day (bpd) in March 2009, down from 2.6 million in 2006. This had devastating economic effects on Shell Petroleum Development Company (SDPC), such that by March 2009, production from its onshore business had plunged to 300,000bpd, down from nearly one million before the crisis in the region escalated in 2004. The country lost at least $23.7 billion to oil theft, sabotage and shut-in production in the first nine months of 2008, and about 1,000 people were killed within the same period (ICG Policy Briefing, 2009:2).

What is more, the government had initially planned to organise a national summit on the Niger Delta, whose steering committee was to be headed by Professor Ibrahim Gambari, a Nigerian scholar, diplomat and special adviser to UN Secretary-General Ban Ki-moon. The option was presented as a compromise between the government's insistence on keeping the Delta crisis an internal affair and the demands of Delta ethnic leaders and militants for UN or other international mediation (ICG Policy Briefing, 2009:6-7). Although the government considered the summit as crucial to implementing its administration's policies on the Niger Delta, with a promise that the Summit would not be another 'pointless and diversionary jamboree as some fear' (quoted in ICG Policy Briefing, 2009:6), the high level of opposition to the summit, which was predicated upon the existence of reports of several previous committees and study groups, ensured the collapse of the initiative. The opposition to Gambari's nomination was particularly fierce because as Nigeria's UN Ambassador in 1995, he defended the execution of environmental rights activist, Ken Saro- Wiwa and eight other Ogoni by the Abacha dictatorship (ICG Policy Briefing, 2009:7). Establishing the NDTC, consisting of broad representation from the region, therefore, seems a right step in the right direction.

Moreover, the composition of the NDTC adds to its overall credibility. [1] Not only did it cut across the nine states that fall under the distinc-

---

[1]  **The Members of the NDTC, 2008 are:** Ledum Mitee, President of the Movement for the Survival of Ogoni People, MOSOP (Rivers State); Nkoyo Toyo, Executive Director, Gender and Development Action (Cross River State); Prince Tonye Princewill, Action Congress governorship candidate for the 2007 elections (Rivers State); Tony Uranta, Executive Secretary, United Niger Delta Energy Development Security Strategy (Rivers State); Magnus Njei Abe, Secretary to the Rivers State Government (Rivers State); Chibuzor Ugowoha, Total Exploration and Production Nigeria Ltd. (Rivers State); Anyakwee Nsirimovu, Executive Director, Institute of Human Rights and Humanitarian Law, Port Harcourt (Rivers State); Timi Alaibe, Executive Director, Niger Delta Development Commission, NDDC (Bayelsa State); Atei Beredugo, Director of Planning, Niger Delta Development Commission (Bayelsa State); Dr Kalu Idika Kalu, economist, former Minister of Finance, National Planning and Transport (Abia State); Chief Anthony Ani, former Minister of Finance (Akwa Ibom State); Sam Amuka, journalist, publisher of *Vanguard* newspapers (Delta State); Lawrence Ekpebu, Professor of Political Science, former Ambassador and Chairman, Presidential Monitoring Committee on NDDC (Bayelsa State); Austin Ikein, Professor of Business Economics, Finance and Development, Delaware State University, USA (Bayelsa State); Omofume Onoge, Professor of History (Delta State); B. I. C. Ijeoma, Professor of Sociology (Delta State); Peter King, Professor and Fulbright scholar (Delta State); G. M. Umezurike, former Vice Chancellor, Imo State University (Imo State); Julius Ihonvbere, Professor of Political Science, former Special Adviser to President Olusegun Obasanjo (Edo State); Stella Omu, Senator 1999-2003 (Delta State); D. I. Kekemeke, former member of the Ondo State House of Assembly and present Secretary to the Ondo State Government (Ondo State); Nduese Essien, member of the House of Representatives 1999-2007 (Akwa Ibom State); Chief E. C. Adiele (Imo State); Chief Tony Esu, former member of the House of Representatives (Delta State); Chief Isaac Jemide, one time member of the House of Assembly in the old Bendel State, now split into Delta and Edo States (Delta State);

---

tive appellation of the political Niger Delta,[2] but also include leading human rights and environmental justice activists, scholar-activists, journalists, politicians, bureaucrats and public policy makers. After the botched attempt by the government to impose Dr Kalu Idiaka Kalu, a former World Bank economist who had served twice as finance minister and also as national planning and transport minister, as chairman, the NDTC began by constituting its own leadership independently. In the process, Ledum Mitee, president of the Movement for the Survival of Ogoni People (MOSOP) was elected as its chairman and Nkoyo Toyo, a leading civil society activist, as its secretary. These are people of proven integrity and consistent commitment to the Niger Delta struggle.

The activities of the NDTC too, especially its processes were impressive. It began by publishing its terms of reference, divided into eight sub-committees, embarked on national and international consultations and called for memorandum from public. These strategies worked well such that the NDTC, according to the International Crisis Group, was able to as-

---

Chief John Anderson Eseimokumo, chartered accountant, Commissioner representing Bayelsa State in NDDC (Bayelsa State); Chief Olusola Okey, former Chairman, Ondo State Oil Producing Areas Development Commission (Ondo State); Dr Youpele Banigo, lecturer in History, University of Port Harcourt (Bayelsa State); Dr Sam Amadi, former Special Adviser to Senate President Ken Nnamani (Rivers State); Dr Godswill Ihetu, former Group Executive Director (Engineering and Technology), Nigerian National Petroleum Corporation (Edo State); Charles Edosomwan, Senior Advocate of Nigeria, former Attorney General and Commissioner for Justice in Edo State (Edo State); Benard Jamaho, legal practitioner (Cross River State); Cyril Anyanwu, legal practitioner, Special Assistant (SpecialDuties) to the Governor of Imo State (Imo State); Grace Ekong, former Secretary to the Government of Akwa Ibom State (Cross River State); Ukandi Gabriel Ogar, former Head of the Cross River State Civil Service (Cross River State); Ben Boyegha, civil society leader (Edo State); Peter Ebhalemen, retired Rear Admiral (Edo State); Cletus Emein, retired Brigadier General and former military administrator of Niger State (Delta State); Paul Edor Obi, retired Colonel and former military administrator of Rivers State (Cross River State); Wole Ohunayo, retired Colonel (Ondo State); Dr Abel Dafiogho, representative of Niger Deltans in the diaspora, U.S.(Delta State); Ombrai Oguoko, representative of Niger Deltans in the diaspora, UK (Rivers State); Ayebami I. Spiff, Professor of Chemistry (Rivers State). See *International Crisis Group Africa Briefing* N°60, 30 April 2009, p. 20.

[2] There has been a raging debate as to the correct definition of the Niger Delta. Geographically speaking, and historically too, the Niger Delta assumes a different meaning and narrower scope than the current nine states of the Niger Delta Development Commission (NDDC) would suggest. See Omotola, 2009a; Naanen, 1995; 2001.

semble and review over 400 reports, memorandums and other documents from both local and international stakeholders [3]. Interestingly, these entries came from different ethnic nationalities in the country, including the Arewa Consultative Forum (ACF) in northern Nigeria; Afenifere, the pan-Yoruba socio-cultural body in western Nigeria; Ohan'Eze Ndigbo and the Movement for Actualisation of the Sovereign State of Biafra (MASSOB) in the Ibo south east; and oil companies operating in the Delta (ICG Policy Briefing, 2009:7).

The democratic and participatory approach of the NDTC, couple with the quality of its members, may have rubbed positively on the recommendations of the Committee. The recommendations of the NDTC were, like the Ogomudia report, in three phases. The first part was a "Compact with Stakeholders on the Niger Delta". These include: increase immediately the Delta's allocation from oil and gas revenues from the present 13 per cent to 25 per cent, to be dedicated largely to new infrastructure and sustainable development of the region; complete within six months initial steps to support a process for disarming youths involved in militancy, including a comprehensive ceasefire and pull-back of forces; bail (with a view to an eventual negotiated release) for Henry Okah; credible amnesty conditions; a negotiated undertaking by militant groups to stop all kidnappings, hostage taking and attacks on oil installations; and formation of a Demobilisation, Disarmament and Rehabilitation (DDR) Commission. Others are to improve the operational integrity of security forces and police in the Niger

---

[3]  Major reports published by the Nigerian government, which the Technical Committee reviewed, included the following: Report of the Commission Appointed to Enquire into the Fears of the Minorities and the Means of Allaying them (1958); The Constitution of the Federal Republic of Nigeria, 1963; Report of the Judicial Commission of Inquiry into Cause of Fuel Shortages in Nigeria, 1992; Report of the Ministerial Fact-Finding Team to Oil Producing Communities in Nigeria, 1994; Report of the Vision 2010 Committee, 1996; Report of the Presidential Committee on the Development Options for the Niger Delta, 1996; Report of the UN Special Rapporteur on Human Rights Situation in Nigeria, 1997; Report of the Special Security Committee on the Oil Producing Areas, 2001; White Paper on the Report of the Presidential Panel on National Security, 2003;National Political Reform Conference Report, 2005; Niger Delta Human Development Report, UNDP, 2006; Niger Delta Regional Development Master Plan, NDDC, 2006; and Report of the Presidential Council on the Social and Economic Development of the Coastal States, 2006. Source: *International Crisis Group Africa Briefing* N°60, 30 April 2009, p. 20.

Delta sufficiently to assure communities and businesses about their safety; establish by mid-2009, with state and local governments, a Youth Employment Scheme (YES) to give at least 2,000 young people community work in each local government of the nine Niger Delta states; complete by June 2010 the work to turn the East-West Road from Calabar to Lagos into a dual carriageway and the construction of at least a link road to the coast in each state, backed by a fully funded roads maintenance program; ensure by June 2010 a total of 5,000mw of power for the Niger Delta region; strengthen independent regulation of oil pollution, including work towards an effective environmental impact assessment (EIA) mechanism, and end gas flaring by 31 December 2008, as previously ordered by the federal government; and rehabilitate all health care facilities and give free medical care to those 65 and above, children under five, and pregnant women, as well as free drugs to malaria patients (Agbo, 2009:21; ICG Policy Briefing, 2009:8).

The second part of the recommendations laid out broad themes and roles for stakeholders in a regional transformation agenda running, including issues of governance, militancy, rule of law and regional and human development to 2020. The third part recommended ways of implementing the recommendations of the Committee. Specifically, it charges the federal government to create institutions and mechanisms to see to the effective implementation of the Compact. The recommended institutions and mechanisms were: National Minority Commission, to deal with minority and micro-minority issues; a Multi-Stakeholder Niger Delta Policy and Project Compliance Monitoring Committee, to monitor the implementation of the Compact and longer-range recommendations; a Niger Delta Special Infrastructural Development Fund, to receive contributions from federal and state governments, oil companies, donors and others; a Niger Delta Futures Trust Fund, for developing agriculture and industries outside the oil and gas sector; and a Community Trust Fund for Oil Producing Communities, to allow communities to share in the wealth in their territories (Agbo, 2009:26).

## 7.5. The limits of a report

On the whole, there is no gainsaying the fact that the report of the NDTC is comprehensive and far reaching. If well implemented, it harbours a lot of potentials for the speedy resolution of the Niger Delta question. However, there are also reasons to be sceptical about its potentials. Indeed, there are limited possibilities to reason otherwise. First, most of the recommendations of the NDTC bothers on fiscal federalism, which is not only a constitutional matter, but also a vex issue in Nigeria's convoluted federalism (Aiyede, 2009). Effecting any serious alteration to the existing order may require constitutional changes, or at least a national consensus through a national conference. Given the advantages and disadvantages that will come with such changes for the ethnic minorities of the Niger Delta and the 'others' especially the majorities, respectively, such adjustments will not easily come by[4]. Similar disagreements between the Niger Delta and the ethnic majorities, particularly the Northern Hausa-Fulani, crippled the 2005 NPRC, forcing it into an unceremonious end (Saliu and Omotola, 2008). Nothing fundamental seems to have changed.

Second, it is a while now that the NDTC had submitted its reports to the government, precisely on 1 December 2008. Ever since, the government has not lifted a finger in the direction of implementation, not even in the form of issuing a white paper. There is already palpable fear that another committee would be set up to review the report of the NDTC. Ledum Mitee, who chaired the NDTC, quoting Ufot Ekaette, the Minister of Niger Delta Affairs, expressed the worry in a recent interview with *Tell*, a leading weekly Nigerian magazine thus:

You know, as I always say, the ways of government passeth (sic) my understanding. There are certain things (on which) you thought the government should hit the ground running, but what I heard, and you must have heard, from the minister of the Niger Delta Ministry, he was in press recently, is that a white paper committee is now being set up to review the report. So, apparently, I know that after the committee another committee will be set up to review the committee's own recommendations and eventually the executive will review it and so on ... to infinity (Mitee, 2009: 22).

Yet, Nigerians especially the Niger Deltans are still waiting for the white paper, not to talk of the commencement of its execution.

---

[4] Again, the Yar'Adua government has a reputation for slowness. In such a situation, even if the government accedes to such demands (a remote possibility, anyway), it will take some time for it to materialize.

Moreover, there have been several committee reports in the past, which received little or no attention from the government. As already indicated earlier, fourteen (14) of such reports exist prior to the setting up of the NDTC. Most of these reports particularly the Ogomudia Report of 2002 made far reaching recommendations that would have helped address the Niger Delta question in no small measures. The failure to implement these reports may not be unconnected to the opportunity the Niger Delta problem offers political leaders at all levels as a domain of enforcing domination and further exploitation of the already traumatised vulnerable groups, most especially women and youths. In other words, the continuation and compli-cation of the Niger Delta question offers unparallel opportunities for primi-tive accumulation of capital, including official corruption. Finding a lasting solution to the problem, therefore, amounts to reducing, if not denying in its entirety, the captive territory of elite primitive accumulation of wealth. A solution to the Niger Delta problem will, also, not serve the interests of the oil multinationals and the so-called liberation movements/militias in the region. The cry for a lasting solution from all stakeholders may be hypo-critical, after all.

Furthermore, the establishment of the Ministry of the Niger Delta on 10 September 2008, barely a week after the announcement of the NDTC, speaks volume about the insincerity of the government regarding the lat-ter. In fact, the creation of the ministry to be responsible for development projects in the region, including roads, electricity and other utilities, pre-viously executed by multiple ministries, in order to provide better focus and quick implementation and to demonstrate commitment to the Delta, raises more questions than answers. For one, it was not only pre-judicial, but also pre-emptive of the NDTC. Second, it may bring about counter-agitations for separate ministries by other regions affected by one problem or the other. In the recent past, for example, the creation of the Oil Min-eral Producing Area Development Commission (OMPADEC) led to the agitation for Hydro-Power Area Development Commission (HIPADEC). More importantly, what will be the exact relationship between the ministry and the NDTC remains undefined, posing itself a potential source of con-flict of interests and personalities. This singular act, more than anything else, suggests that the government was not sincere with the composition of the NDTC. The original design may be to highjack the leadership of the

NDTC, through which the government could manoeuvre its way and work to a designated conclusion. The popular resistance to this and the eventual emergence of Ledum Mitee, a renowned human rights and environmental activist, may have forced the almost immediate search for alternative. The creation of the ministry of the Niger Delta offers one. By implication, setting the NDTC was, from the outset, a ploy to buy legitimacy for further exploitation of the Niger Delta.

Subsequent events in the region attest to this claim. The most eloquent testimony to date is the ongoing war between the JTF and militant movements in the region. While criminality in whatever guise needs to be confronted frontally, the form of its delivery helps reveal the real intention of the government. The sophistication of arms and ammunition deployed, the level of destruction done so far, including violation of the basic rights of the people especially women, children and the aged, represent critical violations of the law of just war. The JTF owes it a responsibility to protect civilian population and respect their rights in all ramifications. So far, this has not been the case, exemplified by the increasing number of displacement and rising refugee flows in the region. It is on these notes that the prospects of the NDTC in addressing the Niger Delta question are gloomy. As Agbo (2009:19) concludes:

The report of the Technical Committee on the Niger Delta holds a lot of promise for the resolution of the crisis in the region, but the government may not implement the key recommendations because of the "national question," thus further endangering the goose that lays the golden egg.

## 7.6. The challenges ahead: a conclusion

The establishment of the NDTC was a harbinger of hope. The composition of the Committee, its leadership and democratic cum participatory approach helped add glowing light to these expectations. The depth of the report, both in terms of recommendations and implementation strategies, only served to introduce another dimension of expectations. Together they gave the impression that a lasting solution to the deepening contradictions of the region was in the pipeline. But as it has turned out, such hopes hinged on the NDTC vis-à-vis the Niger Delta question may have been effectively squandered. As the preceding analyses suggest, the initiative seems to have been permanently caught between hope and despair. Some notable contra-dictions, which demean the continue appeal of the initiative and by exten-sion its overall potentials to contribute to the resolution of the Niger Delta question include, among others, the fact that so far nothing concrete has been done about the report since its submission; the pre-emptive creation of a Ministry of the Niger Delta, barely two weeks after the inauguration of the NDTC, suggests that the government already had a mind-set on the issue, and the often lack of political will on the past of successive Nigerian governments to implement previous reports on the Niger Delta. From all indications, nothing suggests that the Yar'Adua government would be dif-ferent. The way the electoral reform process has been botched, epitomised by the rejection and subsequent removal of the core and most important recommendations of the election reform committee from the white paper on the report, is indicative of the low level of political will attributable to the Yar'Adua government.

The import of this is that there are future challenges to be confronted, with both research and policy implications. The challenges include what and how to find a lasting solution to the Niger Delta problem that will be acceptable to all stakeholders in the Nigerian federation. This calls for iden-tifying why previous efforts have not yielded the desired resort. While the causes of the failure of some of the previous efforts are institutional, be-havioural and attitudinal, the nature of national and local leadership seems central. So, also, the task of neutralising criminals that have polluted an otherwise justifiable cause, without necessarily militarising the region, as is currently the case. Indeed, the current military onslaught may create a backlash of unintended consequences. These include the possible dispersal of militants/fighters beyond the region to temporarily safe havens across the country. Such an occurrence poses more serious and wider security threats for the country and the world at large. In the process, the militants may begin an aggressive search and recruitment of converts all over, filling then with ideological socialisation and insurgent trainings, as well as building in-ternational networks. They may also resort to insurgent/terrorist tactics that will be much more difficult to deal with. What is more, even the so-called JTF and other official actors in the Niger Delta question have been accused of complicity, having seen the protracted conflict as an opportunity to en-rich themselves. As long as such opportunities for predation and primitive accumulation of capital continue to exist, no amount of committee reports can help undo the trend. These are the main challenges that should be the focus of further research, advocacy and public policy.

## 7.7. References

Adaka Boro Centre (2008) The Ogomudia Committee Report. Posted on 14 June 2008. Available at http://www.adakaboro.org/ndtc2008/37-articles/76-theogomudiarep?format=pdf. Accessed on 01/06/2009.

Agbo, A. (2008), 'Niger Delta Betrayed Again', *Tell*, 22 December, Lagos, pp. 19-21.

Agbo, A. (2009), 'National Question and the Goose that Lays the Golden Egg', *Tell*, 16 March, Lagos, pp. 19-23.

Akinyele, R. T. (1996), 'States Creation in Nigeria: The Willink Report in Retrospect', *African Studies Review*, 39, No. 2, pp. 71-94

Ayoade, John A. (2008), Submission at a recent Nigerian Country Roundtable on Diversity and Unity in Federal Countries, Department of Political Science, University of Ibadan, coordinated by Professor Rotimi Suberu of the same department – under the Forum of Federations and International Association of Centres for Federal Studies' (IACFS) A Global Dialogue on Federalism, 17 January, 2008. This author was one of the participants at the Round table.

Ekpebu, Larry (2008), "The State, Oil Companies and the Niger Delta: Keynote Speech", In *Proceeding of the International Conference on the Nigerian State, Oil Industry and the Niger Delta* (PICNSOIND), *Wilberforce* Island: Department of Political Science, Niger Delta University (NDU), 2008, pp. 4-11.

Goodluck, J. (2008), Address by Dr. Goodluck Ebele Jonathan, GCON, Vice President of the Federal Republic of Nigeria on the occasion of the inauguration of the Technical Committee on the Niger Delta, 8th September, 2008. Available at http://www.nigerdeltatechnicalcommittee.org/index.php?option=com_content&view=article&id=47&Itemid=57. Accessed on 01/06/2009.

International Crisis Group (2009). Nigeria: Seizing the Moment in the Niger Delta. *International Crisis Group Africa Briefing* N°60, 30 April.

Kaladumo, C.O.K. (1996), 'The Implications of Gas Flaring on the Niger Delta Environment', Paper Presented at the 8th International Seminar on the Petroleum Industry and the Nigerian Environment, Port Harcourt, 18-21 November.

Kaladumo, C.O.K. (1996), 'The Implications of Gas Flaring on the Niger Delta Environment', Paper Presented at the 8th International Seminar on the *Petroleum Industry and the Nigerian Environment*, Port Harcourt, 18-21 November, 1996.

Naanen, Ben (1995), 'Oil Producing Minorities and the Restructuring of Nigerian federalism: The case of the Ogoni People', *Commonwealth and Comparative Politics*, 31 (1).

Naanen, Ben (2001), 'The Niger Delta and the National Question', in Osaghae, Eghosa E. and Ebere Onwudike (eds.) *The Management of the National Question in Nigeria* (Ibadan: The Lord's Creation, for Programmes on Ethnic and Federal Studies, PEFS).

O'Neil, Tom (2007), 'Curse of the Black Gold: Hope and Betrayal in the Niger Delta', *National Geographic*, 211, 2.

Okonjo-Iweala, Ngozi, Charles Soludo and Mansur Muhtar (2003), 'Introduction', (eds.) *The Debt Trap in Nigeria: Towards a Sustainable Debt Strategy*, Trenton, NJ: Africa World Press.

Omotola, J. S. (2006), *The Next Gulf? Oil Politics, Environmental Apocalypse and Rising Tensions in the Niger Delta*, ACCORD Occasional Paper Series, 1 (3).

Omotola, J. S. (2007), 'From the OMPADEC to the NDDC: An Assessment of State Responses to Environmental Insecurity in the Niger Delta', *Africa Today*, 54 (1), pp. 73-89.

Omotola, J. S. (2008), ' "Liberation Movements" and Rising Violence in the Niger Delta: The New Contentious Site of Oil and Environmental Politics', paper presented at the *Wars and Conflicts in Africa Conference*, Department of History, University of Texas at Austin, USA, 28-30 March.

Omotola, J. S. (2009a), 'Dissent and State Excesses in the Niger Delta, Nigeria', *Studies in Conflict & Terrorism*, 32 (2), pp. 129-145.

Omotola, J. S. (2009b), 'From Political Mercenarism to Militias: the Political Origin of Niger Delta Militias', in Ojakorotu, Victor (ed.), *Fresh Dimensions on the Niger Delta Crisis of Nigeria*, Houston and Bangkok: JAPSS Press Inc., pp. 91-124.

Omotola, J. S. (2009c), 'Yar'Adua's Seven Point Agenda in the Context of the Millennium Development Goals', in Albert, Olawale I. (ed), *Scales and Spaces of Political Concepts and Phraseologies in Nigeria under the Fourth Republic: Essay in Honour of Governor Aliyu Babangida* (forthcoming).

Opukri, C.O. and Ibaba, Samuel I. (2008), 'Oil Induced Environmental Degradation and Internet Population Displacement in the Nigeria's Niger Delta', *Journal of Sustainable Development in Africa*, 10, 1 (2008), p. 181.

Opukri, C.O. and Ibaba, Samuel I. (2008), 'Oil Induced Environmental Degradation and Internal Population Displacement in the Nigeria's Niger Delta', *Journal of Sustainable Development in Africa*, 9, (4).

Osaghae, Eghosa E. (1991), 'Ethnic Minorities and Federalism in Nigeria', *African Affairs*, 90, 355.

Osaghae, E. E. (1995), 'Ogoni Uprising: Oil Politics, Minority Agitation and the Future of the Nigerian State', *African Affairs,* 94(376): 325-344.

Osaghae, Eghosa E. (1998), 'Managing Multiple Minority Problems in a Divided Society: The Nigerian Experience,' *Journal of Modern African Studies*, 36, 1, pp. 1-20

Osuoka, Isaac A (2007), 'Oil and Gas Revenues and Development Challenges for the Niger Delta and Nigeria', Paper presented at the Expert Group Meeting on the use of Non-Renewable Resource Revenues for Sustainable Local Development. Organised by the UN Department of Economic and Social Affairs, UN Headquarters, New York, Friday 21 September. Available at http://www.un.org/esa/sustdev/sdissues/institutional_arrangements/egm2007/presentations/isaacOsuoka.pdf. Retrieved on 07/02/2008.

Roberts, Nyemutu F. (2000), *The State, Accumulation and Violence: The Politics of Environmental Security in Nigeria's Oil Producing Areas.* Ibadan: Nigerian Institute of Social and Economic Research (NISER), Monograph Series 17.

Roberts, Nyemutu F. (2000), *The State, Accumulation and Violence: The Politics of Environmental Security in Nigeria's Oil Producing Areas.* Nigerian Institute of Social and Economic Research (NISER), Monograph Series 17.

Saliu, H. A. and Omotola, J. S. (2008) 'The National Political Reform Conference and the Future of Nigerian Democracy', in Saliu, H. A., H. I. Jimoh, N. Yusuf and E. O. Ojo (eds.), *Perspectives on Nation Building and Development in Nigeria: Political and Legal Issues*, Lagos: Concept Publications/Faculty of Business and Social Sciences, University of Ilorin, pp. 168-196.

UNDP (2006), *Niger Delta Human Development Report*, Abuja, Nigeria: UNDP.

# 8. Nigerian leaders in the 1990s and politics of oil in the Niger Delta

Dr. Victor Ojakorotu and None Louis Morake

## 8.1. Introduction

The violence in the Niger Delta and its effects on the denizens of that region has been the concern of scholars and environment activists for over four (4) decades. However, little efforts have been made to analyse the policies of successive Nigerian leaders as the bane of peace in the region.

The grievances of the communities in the Niger Delta centre on one fundamental issue: that of environmental degradation that is the by-product of oil exploitation, gross marginalisation and total exclusion of the local people from access to oil wealth that has been generated from the region.

Nigeria is the world's sixth-largest oil exporter with billions of dollars accruing to the state yearly through oil produced from the Niger Delta region. But, this does not translate to physical development of the Niger Delta, which generates more than eighty (80) per cent of national wealth. The perceived insensitivity of the state and oil multinationals to the plight of the oil-bearing communities has informed the recurrence of violence in different dimensions with serious consequences on both the women and children of the region. For four (4) decades, the men and women of the region have adopted the violent method to change the policies of the state and the foreign oil multinationals without success. Given the complexity of the conflict and its challenges to the unity of the state, it is pertinent to examine the policies of the Nigerian leaders towards the region in the 1990s and their implication for peace.

What marks Nigeria out in a unique fashion is the extreme turbulence that has characterised the state since 1960 and the Niger Delta crisis is at the fore. This recurring conflict can be managed, though. Integral to the crisis in the Niger Delta and by extension the other problematique in the Nigerian state, *inter alia*, is the perceived lopsidedness in the country's federal system. The anomalies in the Nigerian federal arrangement, exemplified for instance by the overarching power of the central government and the lack of real autonomy at the state level, have been a factor in the unfolding of the Niger Delta crisis. The practice of true federalism, which is expected to guarantee local governance structures and communities a measure of control over certain matters that affect them, has been a major issue in the contestations regarding the structure of the Nigerian state. More importantly, the manner in which Nigeria is presently constituted impinges on the situation in the Niger Delta – a region inhabited mainly by those popularly described as ethnic minorities. The perceived non-involvement of the people of the Niger Delta in crucial decision-making and policy implementation organs – partly derived from Nigeria's ersatz federalism – has engendered alienation on the part of the oil minorities thereby leading to virulent expressions of frustration.

It is pertinent to point out at the outset that the internationalisation of the Niger Delta crisis has been facilitated by certain actors within the context of globalisation in which case events in any one country are not only seen in farthest regions of the world but, also, they elicit international reactions. The actions or inactions (militarization and violation of the host communities' rights) of the Nigerian state, the oil multinationals, social movements in the Niger Delta as well as those of international non-governmental organisations have pushed the Niger Delta crisis to the forefront of international environmental discourse.

Perhaps no other phenomenon has launched the region to the forefront of international environmental discourse as the impact of oil politics on the people of the Niger Delta[1]. As have been shown in academic discourse, oil exploration by multinational corporations has brought with it a number of economic, social and environmental consequences that are mostly negative. More often than not, social movements as well as local and international environmental rights activists have predicated their advocacy on the deleterious effects of oil multinationals' activity in the Niger Delta. The internationalisation of the crisis in the region has therefore drawn from the consequences of oil exploration. In fact, the negative effects of oil activities

---

[1] The internationalisation of the Niger Delta crisis have been discussed exhaustively by one of the authors in his doctoral dissertation titled "The internationalisation of Domestic Crisis: A case study of the Niger Delta 1993-2003)

have been at the heart of the campaign for addressing the environmental problems in the region. It is also trite to say that the consequences of oil exploration have evoked international reactions in a manner that typifies the internationalisation of the issues pertaining to the Niger Delta.

However, two of the prominent social movements in the Niger Delta in the 1990s – the Movement for the Survival of the Ogoni People (MOSOP) and the Ijaw Youth Congress (IYC) – have conducted their agitation for undoing the ecological damage to the region in such a way that attracted international attention. MOSOP's strategies of advocacy, lobby and mobilisation of actors and environmental activists within the international community as well as IYC's violent struggles, sometimes, have combined to push the Niger Delta problematic to levels beyond the scope of the Nigerian state. Their engagement with the problems confronting the region have reverberated beyond the borders of the Nigerian state in which case global state and non-state actors have been drawn into what could have been Nigeria's internal affairs, *stricto sensu*. Hence, the disposition of social movements towards the situation in the region, their *modus operandi* and the plausible effects of their actions (e.g. hostage taking) have been a factor in the internationalisation of the crisis in the Niger Delta. The strategies adopted by the social movements in their resistance against the Nigerian state and the oil multinationals and the responses they have provoked from the state and the oil conglomerates suggest that the region's resistance was not without some form of counter-reaction from both the Nigerian government and the multinational oil companies. Social movement activity and the repression of resistance have precipitated a deplorable human rights situation in the Niger Delta. These have, in turn, attracted the attention of the international community which is (generally speaking) seized on the promotion of these rights. Therefore, the role of the military leaders and incumbent civilian regime in the state deserve scholarly attention.

## 8.2. The military leaders, oil and ethnic minorities of the Niger Delta

The Nigerian state has witnessed more of military rule than a civilian democratic arrangement of any sort and this, of course, has implications on the Niger Delta as well. It is very important to mention the fact that the regimes of Generals Ibrahim Badamosi Babangida and Sani Abacha were very repressive, and they violated human rights (the Umuchem fiasco and the hanging of Ken Saro-Wiwa) in the region and the country as a whole. These regimes also deepened the contradictions and crises of the Nigerian state with their policies in the late 1980s and 1990s as power was concentrated in the hands of very few through their system of prebendalism. Thus, these individuals promoted ethnic tension through the use of the ethnic factor in the distribution of social goods and scarce resources, invariably resulting in polarisation and division among ethnic groups in the country. For instance, there were unprecedented inter-ethnic, religious and communal conflicts between the 1980s and the 1990s. Said Adejumobi captures the foregoing in the following words:

From the North to the South, communities and religious groups, which had hitherto lived together in harmony, suddenly took up arms against each other. ... , while virtually all the oil producing communities of the Niger Delta were the epicentres of communal conflicts. [2]

As far back as 1966, the Nigerian state under Major General Aguiyi Ironsi opted for unitary system of government with severe implication for revenue allocation principles of derivation and nationality as it became treasonable to agitate for such ideas. To suppress popular dissent that grew in response to the mismanagement of resources by the military, there was a massive high handed counter response in which the government demonstrated that it would not tolerate the agitation of the oil minorities of the Niger Delta. [3] The Adaka Boro revolution of 1966 was the first major case in this direction. Its revolution that lasted for almost 12 days was aimed at proclaiming and establishing an independent Niger Delta Republic, but this attempt was thwarted by the Federal Military Government. The revolutionists were subsequently tried for treason and later sentenced to death.

On the other hand, the trial and hanging of the Ogoni 9 by the military regime of General Sani Abacha drew the attention of the international

---

[2]   S. Adejumobi, Ethnic Militia Groups and the National Question in Nigeria, Social Science Research Council Working Papers, March 2003.

[3]   O. Oyerinde, "Oil, Disempowerment and Resistance in the Niger Delta" in O. Olorode *et al, Ken Saro-Wiwa and the Crises of the Nigerian state* CDHR, Lagos, 1998, pp. 63-64

community to the plight of the oil rich Niger Delta of Nigeria. The action of the Nigerian government was aimed at suppressing the agitations and disruption of oil production in Nigeria, but it led to the explosion of social movements in the region with objectives similar to those of the Movement for the Survival of Ogoni People (MOSOP). Their protest led to the establishment of the Niger Delta Development Board, the Oil Mineral Producing Areas Development Commission (OMPADEC) and much more recently, the Niger Delta Development Commission (NDDC) but the extent to which these organisations were or have been able to address the needs of the region is another controversial issue. Therefore, the struggle of the oil minorities for over four (4) decades hinges on the National Question and this practically involves the issues of minority ethnic groups and how their rights could be accommodated within the Nigeria state. It is on this note that the Federal Government should appreciate the underlying inequalities in order to avoid the persistent conflicts in the region.

It is very important to note that federalism recognises the right and differences of all the ethnic minorities within a state, but as Usman Bugaje argues, "[if] the essence of federalism is to recognise and appreciate our cultural and religious diversity and therefore the differences in our value systems and worldviews, we have already destroyed it by our straight jacketing and regimentation in matters of law, economy and politics..."[4]

In attempting to tackle the problem of the minorities in the Niger Delta within the context of Nigerian federalism, the military took some remarkable steps in order whittle down the impact of the dominant ethnic groups on the minorities in the areas of local government and states creation. However, the extent to which these steps resolved the issue of the minorities is questionable. Bugaje contends, again, that:

The proliferation of states and local governments will not be of any avail, for as long as it is not accompanied with an autonomy, which will allow for a substantial reflection of local culture and values. Our federalism is to say the least phantom and the local autonomy evidently bogus.[5]

Yet this development did not address the demands of the people as it was mere attempt to maintain flow of oil.

---

[4]     U. Bugaje, "Questioning the National Question", *Citizen*, 5 October, 1992
[5]     U. Bugaje, "Questioning the National Question", *Citizen*, 5 October, 1992

## 8.3. Democratic setting and resource control agitation in the Niger Delta

There is no denying the fact that civil agitation of which, ethnic violence is one, would become more prominent under a democratic government in Nigeria. This is so because the military had suppressed such voices through repression. For the Niger Delta crisis to have gained renewed vigour during the Obasanjo administration was, therefore, expected. Ethnic violence is a legacy bequeathed to the democratic government of President Olusegun Obasanjo by the Nigerian military in May 1999. The alarming rate it has assumed, since then, calls for prompt attention and urgent solutions in order to move the nation forward. Despite every effort by the state to address the ugly situation in the region, the tempo of resource control agitation has increased among the people and leaders of the various states in the region.

There was a general assumption that the enthronement of democracy in Nigeria will automatically translate to demilitarisation and development of the Niger Delta as it was also assumed for other regions as well. This position arose from the opportunity that would be provided by entrenchment of the rule of law and other institutions associated with democratic regimes. While it is true that the Obasanjo administration has improved on its predecessors' policies in the Niger Delta, the initial action of the government, especially the 'Odi Massacre', created a dent in the regime's policy toward the region. Notwithstanding the Odi episode, in other areas like the Warri crisis, the legal battle between the littoral states and the central government, and the onshore and offshore debacle, the Nigerian state policy towards the local people has improved considerably.

The action of the president in his first month in office established his sympathy for the region through a draft Bill that established the NDDC. The president thus demonstrated the need to urgently address the plight of the region; this effort, invariably, paid off with the take off of the Commission as an intervention agency to facilitate development in the region. It cannot be safely concluded, though, that the desired development signs are there yet. Nonetheless, with the NDDC in place, government development efforts are now more streamlined and focused.

Moreover, the ineffectiveness of the Commission to effectively discharge its statutory duties is partly related to its inability to secure the necessary funding. It was noted by the Nigerian Senate that the foreign oil multinationals were reluctant to contribute the required 3% of their annual budget to the body; on the side of the central and state governments, there are backlogs of their financial commitment to the Commission. Therefore it is likely that the ideas behind the establishment of the body are far from being fulfilled.

Similarly, the composition of the governing council of NDDC witnessed a huge protest in 1999 from the youths because there is an unsettling conviction that the NDDC would fail like the defunct OMPADEC that enriched few individuals to the detriment of the populace. Their argument stemmed from the involvement of the governors and other bureaucratic bottlenecks in the operation of the body. Given this uncertainty, the deputy director of Environmental Rights Action (ERA) insisted that the organisation would be politicised and drift from the part of addressing the fundamental issues of resources control, self-determination and environmental protection. Notwithstanding, the Commission prides itself as having achieved considerable success in the Niger Delta. As at 2003 the organisation had executed some notable projects in the region as could be seen in the table below.

| PROJECTS | UNITS EXECUTED |
|---|---|
| Roads | 40 |
| Water | 90 |
| Electricity | 129 |
| Shore Protection/Jetty | 47 |

Source: www.nddconline.org/Projects/rebuilding.shtml

Apart from these mentioned projects, the body also undertook some major projects in the area of erection of school buildings, the supplies of educational, agricultural, fishing and hospital equipment. As part of its impact on health infrastructure in the region, it donated an ambulance and X-ray facilities worth millions of naira to the General Hospital in Calabar. The NDDC has built a number of health centres, doctors' and nurses' quarters and donated ambulances to specialist hospitals in other parts of the region.

According to the body (NDDC), as at 2003, a total of 127,148 patients were given free quality medicare, 478 received eye surgeries, 2,683 had general and gynaecological surgeries, 19,490 received free eye-glasses and 4,497 had dental surgeries [6].

Prior to the formation of the NDDC, majority of the people of the oil-bearing communities in the Niger Delta had to rely almost exclusively on traditional medical treatment save for the existence of a few primary health centres managed by the local or state governments. The multinational companies also operated a few, barely equipped hospitals scattered across the Niger Delta. Little wonder that the initiatives by the NDDC in reversing the trends of the past have been commended by a number of people [7]. However, it may be argued that the community projects embarked upon by the NDDC need not draw any special applause from the people given that the Commission was just doing what the state should have been doing all along. The arguments and counter-arguments notwithstanding, some observers have commended the NDDC for its efforts at addressing the problems in the Niger Delta.

It was in recognition of NDDC's efforts at developing the Niger Delta that the organisation was awarded an International Award by European Marketing Research Centre, EMRC, Brussels, Belgium on 15 December 2003. At the presentation ceremony the Director of EMRC, Professor Mathijsen praised the efforts of NDDC for its "spirit of initiative in developing a region that is key to Nigeria's economic fortunes" and that, if the organisation is properly encouraged and financed, it will truly make a difference in the lives of the poverty ridden region. [8]

President Olusegun Obasanjo, also, established a new federal ministry that would address one of the major problems facing the people of the Niger Delta (Ministry of Environment). His regime established the Environmental Monitoring Committee under the Ministry of Environment and appointed "a youth director" for the directorate of Youths Development in the NDDC. The president has signed into law a bill abrogating the dichotomy between onshore and offshore that sparked up a heated debate in Nigeria.

---

[6]　See http://www.guardiannewsngr.com/news/article31 1 April 2004
[7]　The NDDC in the Eyes of the people, TELL Magazine, 7 April, 2003.
[8]　NDDC. "NDDC wins International Award". Press Release No. 1 of 5 January 2004

A series of administrative panels were raised at the local and national levels to proffer solutions into the crisis in the Niger Delta. In a similar vein, these oil companies operating in the Niger Delta have made considerable progress in recent years in their efforts to address the impacts of their operation on the health of the local people in the Niger Delta. It was to this effect that Shell and Africare signed a partnership agreement to establish a $4.5 million health care programme in Nigeria in 2003. The focus of this partnership is to reduce child and maternal mortality from malaria and in order to compliment government efforts in her Roll Back Malaria programme. The company has also been involved in the building of clinics and hospitals in various parts of their area of operations in the Niger Delta.

It is also instructive to note that Shell has been of assistance to the NDDC in the discharge of the Commission's duties. In 2003, Shell contributed some $54.5 million to the NDDC[9]. This is in addition to Shell's direct community development interventions which supplanted the company's community assistance programmes in 1998.

Conclusively, it is right to infer that oil threatens the unity of the state; therefore, Nigerian leaders must carefully address the demands of the host communities rather than pursuing repressive policies. The struggle is becoming more militant in spite of the repression of social movements and destruction of some towns in the Niger Delta.

## 8.4.  Reference

Adejumobi, S. Ethnic Militia Groups and the National Question in Nigeria, Social Science Research Council Working Papers, March 2003.

Bugaje, U. "Questioning the National Question", *Citizen*, 5 October, 1992

Guardian, The. http://www.guardiannewsngr.com/news/article31 1 April 2004

NDDC. "NDDC wins International Award". Press Release No. 1 of 5 January 2004

Oyerinde, O. "Oil, Disempowerment and Resistance in the Niger Delta" in O. Olorode *et al, Ken Saro-Wiwa and the Crises of the Nigerian state* CDHR, Lagos, 1998, pp. 63-64

Shell's Annual Report for 2003 entitled "People and the Environment", p. 18

TELL Magazine.The NDDC in the Eyes of the people, TELL Magazine, 7 April, 2003.

---

[9]    See Shell's Annual Report for 2003 entitled "People and the Environment," p. 18

# 9. The democratisation of violence in the Niger Delta of Nigeria, 1999-2007

J.M. Ayuba

## 9.1. Introduction

The Niger Delta has for some years been the theatre of major confrontations between youth gangs and the Nigerian government security forces, resulting in many deaths and the disruption of oil production. With the inception of democratic rule in 1999 after 28 years of military dictatorship in Nigeria, the Niger Delta has been experiencing an escalation in violence, which is now threatening the security and survival of the country. This paper posits that the concentration of economic and political powers in the Niger Delta states of Bayelsa, Delta, Cross Rivers, Rivers, Ebonyi and Akwa Ibom means that the states have become a terrain of struggle and conflict for the control of resources between opposing groups. Since 1999, politicians in the region have been hiring youth gangs to rig elections in the various states. These gangs have since become a thorn in the flesh of both the federal government of Nigeria and innocent people in the region.

## 9.2. A history of political violence in the Niger Delta

The most worrying aspect of the conflict in the Niger Delta is that the region is being transformed into something more akin to the American gangland fights for control of the drug trade. The increase in violence in the region has highlighted more profound national challenges now facing the government. Despite the 13 per cent growth in oil revenues from the Niger Delta states, the region remains desperately poor and has high levels of unemployment. The unemployed youths are being hired and armed by politicians to unleash terror in the name of rigging elections. The uncontrolled supply of arms for the struggle over political control into the already volatile Niger Delta has turned the region into one of the most dangerous places in the world. According to security analysts in the Global Services Report of 2003, with over 1000 fatalities every year, it ranked the violence in the Niger Delta alongside that of Chechnya and Colombia. The effort by the Yar'adua government to bring peace to the region hangs in the balance even before any meaningful progress has officially begun.

Local resistance to oil exploration in the region has been transformed from the peaceful protests of the 1970s and 1980s to violent confrontations of the late 1990s up to 2008. The increase in violence has been exacerbated by the global increase in oil prices and, also, by the arming of gangs by politicians to rig elections between 1999 and 2007. Ogwugah has identified four distinct phases of resistance in the Niger Delta based on the dominant strategies in each phase. [1]

In the first phase, between the early 1970s and the mid 1980s, local communities directed their demands towards the oil companies, and by appealing to the state and by resorting to legal action. However, these strategies failed as oil companies at worst refused to abide by court rulings or at best, paid out some compensation to local communities.

The second phase, between the mid 1980s and the mid 1990s, was characterised by peaceful demonstrations and the occupation of oil installations. The oil companies responded by securing the intervention of the mobile police force and soldiers, which resulted in the destruction of lives and properties. The use of brute force, by both the oil companies and government security agents, to suppress local protests set the stage for subsequent violence in the region. The authoritarian nature of the military junta of Ibrahim Babangida, coupled with the economic downturn of the 1980s, increased the political tension between the oil producing communities and the government. Oil extraction under SAP increased the tension because local people were unable to find expression within the defined political space and, suffering from the harsh consequences of the adjustment, increasingly resorted to violence. [2]

The third phase, between the mid 1990s and 1998, witnessed a rise in violent confrontations between the local communities in the Niger Delta

[1] Ogwuha, Lemmy, "Phase of Resistance in the Niger Delta," *CASS Newsletter* 6 (1999), 5-6.
[2] Obi, Cyril, "Globalisation and Local Resistance: The Case of Ogoni versus Shell," *New Political Economy* 2 (1997), 8.

and the oil companies and government after the state execution of Ken Saro-Wiwa and eight other Ogoni activists in 1995.[3] This period witnessed the emergence of militant groups across the region that resorted to the forceful occupation of oil facilities and the kidnapping of oil personnel. In 1998, the then Head of State General Abubakar warned:

> We cannot allow the continued reckless expression of these (angry) feelings. Seizure of oil wells, rigs and platforms, as well as hostage taking, vehicular hi-jacking, all in the name of expressing grievances, are totally unacceptable to this administration.[4]

During the latest phase from 1998 to the present day, emerging militant groups changed the nature of the demands made by the activists of the earlier protest movements in the Niger Delta. Following the Kaiama Declaration in December 1998, the emphasis has shifted from demand for development to that of resource control.[5]

The return to civilian rule in 1999 marked a turning point in the history of violence in the Niger Delta. The nationwide democratic elections in 1999, 2003 and 2007 were undermined by widespread fraud and violence. The Niger Delta is particularly important in the national power structure because territorial control in this region is central to accessing the oil industry and its wealth. Political violence has become a central part of political competition in the Niger Delta region and it takes many forms from assassinations to armed clashes between gangs employed by rival politicians. According to a survey undertaken by Johns Hopkins' School for Advanced International Studies, more than 11,000 Nigerians have lost their lives in clashes along political, ethnic, religious, and other lines between 1999 to the end of 2006 while Nigeria's National Commission for Refugees has estimated that more than three million Nigerians were internally displaced. The violence is most often carried out by gangs recruited and paid by politicians and party leaders to attack their sponsors' rivals, intimidate members of the public, rig elections, and protect their patrons from similar attacks.

---

[3] Ogwuha, "Phase of Resistance."
[4] Quoted by Ayuba, Jonathan, "Oil and Violence in the Niger Delta of Nigeria" (Forthcoming).
[5] Ogwuha, "Phase of Resistance."

Such violence discourages and prevents political participation and plays a central role in denying local people a say in electing their leaders.

Gang violence in the Niger Delta is not a new phenomenon. The region has historically been politically fragmented and it, sometimes, experiences violent disputes over land and fishing rights as well as over the political jurisdictions of local leaders. Violent conflict in the Niger Delta has assumed a more lethal dimension with the deployment of automatic weapons and the employment of superior strategies and tactics using better training and organisation in the 1990s. Increased investments in the mobilisation and organisation of violence has also stemmed from greater stakes and an increasingly conducive atmosphere for violence to thrive. Youth gangs, who were willing and able to protect their villages and elders, became increasingly powerful. As democratic rule returned in 1999, some of these same youths were paid to disrupt political events, provide protection for politicians and were also used to rig elections. Local youths began to look at themselves as the new political opinion leaders as the elders had lost much credibility and respect as a result of corrupt payments from the government and oil companies. The gradual induction of local youths in the Niger Delta into political competition has increased the level of violence and the region is now being held to ransom by different youth gangs or cult members that are backed by politicians.

The notorious cult organisations in the Niger Delta are varieties of criminal gangs that emerged from university campus fraternities and have since proliferated and evolved into violent gangs that often operate both on and off campus with one foot each in the criminal and political spheres. These gangs are the most widely feared criminal enterprises in the region and the power and prevalence of these groups has grown steadily over past decades, especially since 1999. Some of the main centres of cult activities in the Niger Delta are Tombia, Bukuma, Buguma, Okrika, Port Harcourt and Ogbakiri. Cult groups are brutal and secretive and are now taking over whole communities and political structures in the region. Their influence also extends into militias and criminal cartels. Cult gangs are organised as if they were military forces so that it is possible for the top to pass orders down the line. The main sources of funds for arms are drug running, oil bunkering, political patronage, oil company pay-offs and robbery. Many of the cult leaders are associates of government officials and politicians. It is to the process of politicians arming cult members that we now turn in the next paragraph.

In Rivers State, at the heart of Nigeria's restive Niger Delta, the efforts of local politicians to arm and hire criminal gangs to rig elections are out of control. There are around 100 gangs in the oil city of Port Harcourt whose members are said to represent "a standing army of the dispossessed." [6] Rivers is the wealthiest state in Nigeria, with a budget of over N180 billion in 2007. As a result of the relative wealth of the state, there is political competition to gain access to and control of public funds. During the 1999 and 2003 elections, the former governor of Rivers state Peter Odili, with other politicians, hired the Niger Delta People's Volunteer Force (NDPVF) and the Niger Delta Vigilante (NDV), led by Asari Dukobo, and Ateke Tom respectively, to rig the PDP into power in the state. The Niger Delta Vigilante, on the one hand, emerged from the Okrika Vigilante which helped to restore order in Okrika at a time when there were several armed gangs terrorising the Okrika community. Several gangs had laid siege to Okrika levying market women, mourners at funerals, oil bunkerers, petroleum products distributors, commercial motorcyclists and all manner of businesses either legitimate or illegitimate. The emergence of the Niger Delta Vigilante above all these gangs, therefore, brought joy to the people of Okrika who saw the group as providing security and championing their cause. The Niger Delta People's Volunteer Force, on the other hand, was founded in 2004 in an attempt to gain more control over the region's vast oil resources, particularly in Delta State. The NDPVF has, frequently, demanded a greater share of the oil wealth from both the state and federal governments and has occasionally supported independence for the Delta region. The NDPVF's strong Ijaw agenda has led to conflict with the government. The NDPVF began an offensive in October 2004, dubbed "Operation Locust Feast" targeted at oil workers. Demands included multinational companies pumping oil in the Niger Delta to shut down production. However, the group said it would try not to damage the oil installations themselves. After the militants' declaration, international oil prices shot up to more than US $50 a barrel for the first time ever as traders became worried about supplies from Nigeria.

These militia groups (NDPVF and NDV) recruited by Odili were able

---

[6]   *Africa Confidential*, 10 September 2004.

to rig him into power. In an interview conducted by Human Rights Watch in 2007, Ateke Tom acknowledged that he played a vital role in rigging elections in favour of the PDP: "Governor Odili had promised cash and jobs in great quantities for himself and his 'boys' and that in return, 'any place Odili sent me, I conquer[ed] for him. I conquer [ed] everywhere.'" [7] Other gang leaders in the region confirmed Ateke's position:

In 1999 and 2003, [Governor] Odili called us and told us we should work for him. He called other faction leaders of different groups in Port Harcourt. He worked through Asari [Dukobo of the NDPVF] ... They gave some groups N5 million, 3 million, 10 million ... We disrupted the election in favor of our governor and his candidates – we stood at the election ground so people would not come. There was no election. [8]

The militia groups were not only used to rig elections, but also to intimidate members of the opposition party or eliminate those that were perceived as enemies. In a newspaper report:

The National Secretary of the All People's Party (APP), Chief George Moghalu in 2001 accused Mr. Sekibo (special adviser to Odili) of masterminding the killing of an aide to the Ugu/Boro council chairman and, also in concert with local gangs in his payroll, was responsible for the burning of the residences of party stalwarts in the area. [9]

Gang members recruited by politicians to carry out electoral violence were promised more cash payments and patronage after the elections. Much of what was promised to the gangs by the politicians never materialised and this led to a breakdown of relations between many armed groups and their former sponsors. Asari-Dokubo has alleged that they were not properly paid after they had helped the PDP to win the election and in order to fight back they decided to engage in violent activities. [10] There was the fallout, also, between the different gangs, which increased tension and insecurity in the region. According to Amnesty International, the violence of September and October 2004 that claimed over 500 lives represented a falling out amongst

---

[7]   *Human Rights Watch* "Criminal Politics, Violence, "Godfathers" and Corruption in Nigeria, (2007), 36.
[8]   *Ibid.*
[9]   *Thisday*, 2 May 2001.
[10]  See Human Rights Watch Report of 2007.

the gangs and between the gangs and their former political sponsors over the failure of patrons to redistribute the spoils of office. The militant groups now talk the same talk of resource control and self-determination as the leaders of the earlier protest movements. However, they are involved in oil bunkering and other criminal endeavours and have been linked to cult activities. [11]

The violence in the Niger Delta took a dramatic turn for the worse in January 2006 when a new militant group, the Movement for the Emancipation of the Niger Delta (MEND), entered the fray. MEND has been closely linked to the NDPVF and demanded, among other things, the release of Asari and $1.5 billion in compensation from Shell for the pollution they claim it has caused. MEND's first significant act was an attack on Italy's Eni petroleum company. The deaths of nine Eni officials forced the company to evacuate its staff and contractors from the area. Along with further kidnappings and another withdrawal of Shell workers, it was estimated that the instability had resulted in a 10 per cent drop in Nigerian oil production. MEND remain secretive and estimates of its size range from the low hundreds to the low thousands. Like other Niger Delta militant groups, MEND is largely made up of young Ijaw men in their twenties. The group seems to be led by more enlightened and sophisticated men than most of the other groups. Its leaders are educated, some at university level, and they have learned from militant movements in other parts of the world. MEND does not have a united structure but the group is an "idea" more than an organisation and thus, could be compared to a franchise operation or a brand. The movement is able to maintain its secrecy because of sympathy for the group among locals. The leadership of MEND is similarly unclear. Most foreign journalists communicate with Jomo Gbomo, who claims to be a spokesman for MEND. Other group members like Brutus Ebipadei and Major-General Godswill Tamuno have communicated with the press and claimed leadership roles in the group.

The crisis in the Niger Delta has created a booming business of hostage taking for money and storming banks, using arms supplied by politicians during elections. The payment of ransom for the release of hostages, apart

---

[11] Ibeanu, Okey and Luckham, Robin, "Nigeria: Political Violence, Governance and Corporate Responsibility in a Petro-State," in Kaldor, Mary et al, *Oil Wars* (London, 2007), 70.

from benefiting the gangs, has created an avenue for government officials to loot the official coffers by using the excuse of paying for hostage release. The tragic aspect of hostage taking is that, instead of just the oil industry expatriates who were the original targets, it is now affecting affluent families and even local politicians and their relatives. The practice has also begun to spread beyond the Niger Delta to Ondo State on the western fringe of the region and other parts of the country.

The lucrative nature of kidnapping has led to a proliferation of militant groups and a dramatic increase in attacks on both expatriate and local communities, which in turn threatens Nigeria's security. As a result, there is a shift from political protest to a profit venture and the gangs are no longer interested in preserving the long-term viability of Nigeria as an oil exporter. The gangs have also shifted their strategy from the temporary sabotage of infrastructure to threats of permanent destruction of the infrastructure in order to force higher protection payments. [12] The escalation of violence has led to the disruption of Nigeria's oil exports, which has international implications. The strategic importance of the region to the global oil supply makes any unrest in the Niger Delta result in rises in world crude oil prices to historical highs as experienced in June and July of 2008.

## 9.3. The government response to youth militancy in the Niger Delta

The response from politicians who hired these groups has been to take a stronger line against their former supporters. The clampdown has taken many forms. Edo state became the first state in the Niger Delta to sign into law a bill banning the existence and activities of, and membership to, a secret cult when it passed the Secret Cult (Prohibition) Bill in 2000. [13] The law gave the police "sweeping powers ... including the power to 'arrest without warrant any person reasonably suspected of having committed or about to commit an offence under the law.'" [14] This was followed in 2003 by

---

[12] The oil companies and NNPC usually pay some of the militants for protection of pipelines and other oil installations.

[13] *Thisday* 8 December, 2000.

[14] *Ibid.*

the Ebonyi state government, which signed into law a bill aimed at outlaw-ing cults and weapon possession as a means to maintain law and order and protect human rights. [15] In Rivers state, the governor banned 103 secret cult groups through legislation. The Rivers State House of Assembly passed the Secret Cult and Similar Activities (Prohibition) bill in order to check the excesses of the local gangs in the state.

Besides legislation, the government demanded the return of illegal weapons in exchange for money. In June 2007, the government of Rivers under Celestine Omehia, through the Douglas / Needom-led Rivers State Peace and Rehabilitation Committee (RSPRC), announced a plan to award payments of N1 million each to anyone who was willing to renounce vio-lence and surrender their arms. This approach by the government was crit-icised, as the programme did not take into account the integration of gang members into society by providing them with jobs. This "who wants to be a millionaire" promotion provided an opportunity for "criminal gangsters . . . clutching their bibles shouting hosanna in the highest and trooping to Rivers State Government House Chapel as Pentecostal born-again Christians." [16]

In June 2008, the Rivers State Government under Rotimi Amaechi in-augurated the Truth and Reconciliation Commission (TRC) headed by Jus-tice Kayode Eso, to look into the atrocities committed by militants and rec-ommend appropriate amnesty or punishment. The commission had started shakily and was shrouded in controversy when Dr. Odili accused the in-cumbent Governor of witch-hunting. Odili had, thereafter, failed to appear before the Commission at Port-Harcourt saying he was afraid for his life. A special arrangement which saw him appear in Abuja failed to provide answers to the questions posed. At the venue of the Truth and Reconcilia-tion Commission in Abuja, Odili maintained that he had neither sponsored violence nor cult related activities throughout his tenure as the Governor of the state. He denied that he ever was a cult member, ever knew of any cult nor encouraged, supported or financed any cult. He also denied ever arm-ing any person or group to cause violence or mobilise support to achieve electoral victory for himself and the PDP, either in the 1999, 2003 or 2007 general elections in the state. [17] Also, the former Secretary to the State Gov-

---

[15] *Ibid*, 23 December 2003.
[16] *Sahara Reporters*, 11 August 2007.
[17] *Daily Trust* 18 June 2008.

ernment, Dr Abiye Samuel Precious Sekibo, former Deputy Speaker of the House of Representatives, Austin Opara and the immediate past Governor of the state, Celestine Omehia, have since made their positions known at the commission. They absolved themselves of any allegations levelled against them against the backdrop of violence that has engulfed the state. Celestine Omehia broke down in tears while reliving the ordeal his aged mother, Cecilia, went through in the hands of cultists who kidnapped her shortly after his election that was later nullified in court. The major challenge which faced the Commission was the unwillingness of the key militant groups in the region to appear or make any written submission. In fact, Ateke Tom insisted that he had unfinished business with the state governor Amaechi and, therefore, refused to appear before the Eso-led Commission. [18]

The River State Truth and Reconciliation Commission submitted its report in March 2009. The report of the panel went into the root causes of the crises that have been ravaging the state since the return to civilian rule in 1999. The 591 page report highlighted several areas including economy, militancy, multi-national oil companies and cultism. The report indicted the immediate past governor of the state, Dr. Peter Odili, for insensitivity to the plight of the people when the state was under siege by terrorism. The Commission accused the Odili administration of being responsible for creating an atmosphere conducive to the blossoming of cult gangs and aiding the proliferation of arms in the state indiscriminately. According to Justice Eso, it was established that more than 100 cult groups operated in the state, and that Odili's administration, by paying N250, 000.00 per gun submitted to the government, without regard to the gun's age, aided the purchase of more guns and their further proliferation. [19] This helped to engender the series of crises that bedevilled the state during and shortly after the tenure of Odili as governor.

The federal government before its negotiations in April 2006 with MEND refused to enter into any dialogue with militant groups or respond to any of their political demands, instead countering their activities by sending security forces into the Niger Delta. The militant groups have been considered by the federal government as criminal organisations, and the attempt

---

[18]  *Daily Sun*, 4 August 2008.
[19]  *Daily Independent* 23 March 2009.

to quash them with the use of force has exacerbated the security situation in the region. A truce was brokered between the government and MEND in April 2006 and the then president, Olusegun Obasanjo, promised MEND that he would use dialogue and carefully targeted developments to return peace, law, and accountability in government to the impoverished Niger Delta. However, the fragile truce came to a bloody halt in August when soldiers of the Joint Task Force, a contingent of the Nigerian Army, Navy, and Air Force, ambushed 15 members of MEND and murdered them. The men had gone to negotiate the release of a Shell Oil worker kidnapped by youths at Letugbene in a neighbouring community. The incident occurred five days after President Olusegun Obasanjo instructed armed forces commanders in the Niger Delta to resolve the security problems in the region. [20] The government attitude created an atmosphere of suspicion between the militant groups and the federal government throughout the Obasanjo administration.

The coming into office of Yar'adua in May 2007 has changed the Federal Government's approach to the crisis in the Niger Delta. An amnesty deal by the federal government for militants in the region aimed at reducing unrest in the oil-rich region was granted by Yar'adua in June 2009. A presidential pardon, a rehabilitation programme, education and training programmes are being offered to militants taking part in the amnesty programme. [21] The granting of the amnesty was to give peace a chance and to allow development to take place in the Niger Delta. The government argued that for the conditions of the people of the region to improve, and for rapid and meaningful developments to occur the militants must surrender their arms and create an enabling environment for these aims to be achieved. However, barely twelve (12) hours after President Yar'adua proclaimed the amnesty for the militants, MEND blew up a Shell facility at Afremo offshore oil field in Delta State, claiming that its action was in response to the razing down of the homes of some perceived militants at Agbeti community in the state by the Joint Task Force (JTF) on the Niger Delta earlier that day. [22] MEND rejected the offer of amnesty for failing to address some of the concerns of the local people and claimed that the proclamation of

---

[20]  *Thisday,* 21 October 2006.
[21]  *Vanguard,* 25 June 2009.
[22]  *Vanguard,* 27 June 2009.

amnesty seemed to be directed at criminals. According to the spokesperson of MEND, Jomo Gbomo, "if the proclamation was directed at freedom fighters with a cause, it would have addressed the root issues." [23] However, MEND declared a ceasefire in July, shortly after it launched a rare attack on a massive fuel depot in Lagos (the first time the group had carried out such an attack outside the Niger Delta). The ceasefire largely coincided with the 60 day amnesty declared for repentant militants by the government but was later extended after it expired on 15 September 2009 for a further 30 days. [24]

Despite the rejection of the government's offer of an amnesty by MEND, some of the militant groups in the Niger Delta took the opportunity to surrender their arms. In early August 2009, a commander of MEND in Bayelsa state, Mr. Victor Ben (General Boyloaf) led 32 other leaders of militant groups to meet President Yar'adua, where they publicly accepted the amnesty deal offered by the President. [25] Some key militant leaders in the Niger Delta also indicated their interest in accepting the government's amnesty. One of the most feared militants, Chief Government Ekpemupolo (Tompolo) accepted the offer in principle but called on the government to extend the amnesty for the militants by three months. Tompolo argued that the extension of the deadline beyond the initial month of October was necessary in order to ensure that arrangements were made for the care of the militants who surrendered their weapons to the government. [26] The leader of NDV Ateke Tom also accepted the offer of amnesty but stated that he would only surrender his arms outside Rivers state both because of his safety and also a long-standing problem with Governor Amaechi. On his part, Amaechi assured Ateke and other militants in Rivers State, who were yet to embrace the amnesty offered by the government, that no harm would come to them if they surrendered their arms. [27]

Generally, it is too early to gauge the effectiveness of the amnesty offered to the militants to reduce the violence in the Niger Delta. Although some of the senior commanders of MEND and other affiliated gangs in the region have accepted the amnesty, there are other groups that are contin-

[23]   *Daily Trust*, 26 June 2009.
[24]   *Daily Sun*, 16 September 2009.
[25]   *Vanguard*, 7 August 2009.
[26]   *The Nation* 10 September 2009.
[27]   *Thisday*, 13 September 2009.

uing with the armed struggle. However, the declaration of an amnesty by the government and the ceasefire announced by MEND has brought relative peace to the Niger Delta and also increased Nigeria's oil output in the international market.

## 9.4. Conclusion

The return to democratic rule in Nigeria in 1999 has democratised violence in the volatile Niger Delta as politicians contesting for elective offices offered money and arms to youth gangs for electioneering purpose. The widespread use of violence in the politics of the Niger Delta has deprived the local people of the right to vote for their candidates of choice as violence discouraged many voters from coming out to vote. The tragic aspect of violence in the Niger Delta is that the region has been turned into one of the world's most dangerous places. For decades, both the state and federal governments has accrued huge oil revenues, yet the region suffers from a lack of basic infrastructure, with the majority of local youths living in poverty alongside a high level of unemployment. These unemployed youths have become targets of politicians who are using them to achieve their political aims.

# 10. Armed militancy in the Niger Delta: The subtlety of amnesty option and its policy implications for the Nigerian political economy

Dr. Franklins A. Sanubi

## Abstract

*The granting of amnesty by the federal government of Nigeria in June 2009 to armed militants in the Niger Delta provides an ambivalence of policy option in dealing with a tricky politico-economic crisis in the region. Using eufunction as a theoretical framework in analysing the place of the Niger Delta crisis in the political and economic development of the region, the article presents the relevant schools of thought implicit in this policy and defines the subtlety of the federal government policy choice. It concludes with an identification of some policy implications including the level of commitments that all parties will now be required to put towards ensuring peace in the Niger Delta region of Nigeria.*

## 10.1. Introduction and statement of the problem

On Thursday, 25 June 2009 the Nigerian president Umaru Musa Yar'Adua through a national broadcast on the media, made a declaration to the effect of granting unconditional pardon to "all those who have directly or indirectly participated" in the Niger Delta militancy. This amnesty policy, in what has become a show of federal government's good-naturedness and humanitarianism has several serious implications on the political economy of the country.

Emerging from a piecemeal discontent of the local peoples with the federal government's age-long neglect of the region and ignited by a local ethnic crisis in 1996 (Imobighe, 2002) between two minority tribes, the Ijaw and the Itsekiri over a disputed relocation of a newly created Warri-South local government headquarters by the federal government, the Niger Delta Crisis which gave rise to the militancy in the region has for almost two decades now impacted serious reverses on the political economy of the

145

nation. The reverses range from stoppage of oil exploitation activities, intermittent closure of oil wells by major oil companies operating in the area (such as Shell, Chevron, Pan Ocean, Total), blowing up of oil terminals and installations to hostage taking of foreign staff of these oil companies in return for ransom payments amongst other activities. The effects have been very profound: a lull in the nation's oil production and hence in its oil revenues; and, an unprecedented rise in regional insecurity in the Niger Delta with accompanying surge in nationalistic groups in the area purportedly fighting for the rights of the local people in their protests against the federal government development efforts in the region. The growing insecurity in the area has further impacted on the economic lives of the local people as company workers stayed back at home for several months (with the temporary workers among them otherwise known as *contract staff* being frictionally unemployed); domestic production of food plummeting due to fear of insecurity on the farmlands leading to a surge in prices, growing cost of living, and mounting social vices.

The cumulative impact of these crises, notwithstanding, was exacerbated by the proliferation of militant nationalistic groups (albeit criminal outfits) in the region who have found new economic escapades in hostage-talking for ransoms, assassinations, armed robberies and "terror" on the innocent populace. With sharp vagaries in the international prices of crude oil (the country's major export earner) at the heart of a global economic depression (meltdown) continuing with a malnourished national power supply, the economic and social life of the nation let alone the Niger Delta region goes beyond the mere description of a misery or "melancholy". The organic *stress* created by the troubled Niger Delta subsystem into the national economic and political economic system in the wake of this amnesty declaration by the federal government defies category and literal definition. This is the premise under which the implication of the amnesty declaration for the Niger Delta militants on the political economy of the Nigerian state are being analysed.

## 10.2. Amnesty and national development: a conceptual and Nigerian historical perspective

The term amnesty, which probably stems from the Greek word *amnestia*, is a legislative or executive act of oblivion by a government in granting a general pardon or forgiveness to an erstwhile offender. But its usage in political theory has been more often situated in the foreign than in the domestic policy of nations, perhaps because most national offenders often find external escapades upon their perception of self guilt. In particular during the cold war period, national political crises often found support in cold war antagonistic expressions; thus, the involvement of a third party, particularly, a foreign state actor, in such crises pushes them into the realm of international relations between the concerned nations. For instance, during the Nigerian civil war, the rebel leader Odumegwu Ojukwu not only found international friends such as France, Spain, Portugal in the west (Atofarati, 1992), Haiti in Latin America; and some African states such Gabon, Haiti, Côte d'Ivoire, Tanzania and Zambia but also exploited their resources – physical, financial and territorial – in the pursuit of secessionist Biafran irredentist aspiration against Nigeria. In the end, he exiled to one of them. Going slightly beyond the purview of common belief, the application of amnesty to an individual may not necessarily be that such individual has a criminal or offending background. It may in fact be a rethinking of a nation's policy makers on an earlier policy requiring some amendments or corrections. For instance, the term 'amnesty', is being currently floundered in the United States of America before her policy makers as one option to the immigrants' issue of the Obama's administration. The debate on the issue of undocumented immigrants (numbering about 10 million) in the United States in recent years has centred on "what to do with these immigrants" (Cockrail, 2006)... Even the US President Barack Obama (US Immigration Amnesty, 2009) has spoken in support of this policy stating:

We are not going to ship back 12 million people; we're not going to do it as a practical matter. We would have to take all our law enforcement that we have available and we would have to use it and put people on buses, and rip families apart, and that's not who we are, that's not what America is about. So what I've proposed... is you say we're going to bring these folks out of the shadows. We're going to make them pay a fine, they are going to have to learn English, they are going to have to go to the back of the line... but they will have a pathway to citizenship over the course of 10 years.

The ambivalence has been between the view of those who feel that the undocumented immigrants have come to acquire jobs which the American citizens have been denied and of those who feel that the undocumented immigrants have only been invited to take up jobs which the local man would otherwise ignore as meagre and uncivilised. Amnesty policy in this circumstance would be seen as an option for a corrective policy by government, especially as majority of these immigrants have come from countries regarded as belonging to American sphere of influence – from Central and Southern American hemispheres.

The history of amnesty granting in Nigeria began in 1970 under the Yakubu Gowon's regime in his 3Rs (Reconciliation, Reconstruction and Rehabilitation) programme after the civil war to grant an unconditional pardon to all those who supported and or fought on the side of the rebel forces of Biafra in its secessionist struggle against the federal government in the 1967-70 bloody civil war. This was with the view to paving way for peaceful national integration and development after the war. President Shehu Shagari granted amnesty in 1983 to Odumegwu Ojukwu, the leader of the defunct Biafran insurgent military group. Military head of state Abdul Salam Abubakar granted amnesty to detained former Head of State Olusegun Obasanjo in 1999 in an effort to reconcile the various political interests together as the nation geared up for democratic elections in 1999. Olusegun Obasanjo subsequently emerged the president in the 1999-2007 democratic era. President Obasanjo in turn granted amnesty to embattled speaker of the National House of Representatives, Salihu Buhari. A common phenomenon in these amnesties is that they are strongly rooted in political pacification drives of the respective federal government of Nigeria in utter realisation of the nation being a potpourri of differing heterogeneous sub-entities possessing somewhat irreconcilable political and social aspirations. Dinneya (2006:39) has aptly described the precise picture of the transition status of Nigeria's political economy when he writes that:

... the different ethnic nationalities that were banded together for British colonial, administrative convenience have struggled, since political independence in 1960, with the problem of political coexistence as one nation. In the struggle for political control, two broad views have emerged: the nationalists and the ethno-political factions. Ideologically, the former believe that the colonial crafting of the Nigerian nation, with its concomitant pluralism, is in fact not a disadvantage at all, but rather a healthy aid to democratic development. Ethnic politicians on the other hand hold that the Nigerian nation is artificial, very difficult to govern as one nation and, therefore, unworkable as a true democracy

The present slot of amnesty is slightly a departure from the precedent objectives in a response by the federal government to the devastating economic reverse suffered by the nation in the hands of merciless militants.

## 10.3. Eufunctionism, the Niger Delta militancy and the amnesty policy: a theoretical framework

A better theoretical framework, perhaps, for analysing the granting of amnesty to militants in the Niger Delta by the federal government is the framework of eufunctionism. From a sociological parlance and origin, eufunctionism, a variant of functionalism, describes how a process or event, otherwise unnoticed, hidden, and often thought to have a zero or even a negative function yet supportive, strengthens and sustains some latent or even manifest "functions" of a present activity to the benefit and maintenance of order in the subsisting society. Though now an obsolete concept being replaced in modern terms simply by the word "functionalism", eufunctionism describes very vividly how militant activities in the Niger Delta has propagated some of the wishes and aspirations of their "unidentified" sponsors within and without the Niger Delta region in the present policy focus. Militancy did not evolve in isolation. It was structurally designed, resourced and monitored by some unidentified political and social investors with a view to redirecting a federal government's somewhat unacceptable, developmental policy towards the Niger Delta not merely necessarily for the ultimate total benefit of the people of the subsisting community or region but, particularly, and in the immediate perception, the economic and hence political capitulations of these "imaginary" sponsors.

Most of the militants in the Niger Delta would otherwise have been harmless law-abiding citizens seeking lawful means of economic sustenance within the disposition of the national economy. Unfortunately, their ambers of militancy were fanned by the avaricious crop of the political and economic class in the region who saw the opportunities of the precedent economic helplessness on these youths in creating a new form of political and economic adventure in the federal government, perhaps rightly or wrongly. In the course of events, the militants were financed and equipped somewhat sophisticatedly with modern arms, which are, sometimes, more modern than those held by statutory authorities. The "real militants" therefore are not just the physical youths who, being void of any economic or political alternative in the amnesty policy, have been surrendering their arms voluntarily but, in fact, the "unseen" eufuntional investors in this militancy. Implicitly, militancy may have, in some theoretical respect, produced some unexpected results with the amnesty declaration. Director of Nigeria's Institute of Advanced Legal Studies; Prof. Epiphany Azinge, has overtly advised on air, on the national television NTA (26/6/09) that the granting of amnesty in this circumstance should involve an all-inclusive process whereby consideration is given to all interests including those of the sponsors, who may otherwise source other alternative avenues such as recruiting new crop of militants for fresh adventures.

## 10.4. Some policy implications of the federal government's amnesty to Niger Delta militants

Two schools of thought would view the federal government's amnesty policy for the Niger Delta militants from an ambivalent perspective. One school, apparently from a state-centric or nationalistic standpoint, views the policy as a reneging of government's unlimited role in sustaining national security in the face of adversity. National security ranks probably highest, in the ladder of a nation's core or primary interests and no nation, no matter how poorly disposed militarily, would compromise it under any circumstance. From this school of thought, it would appear that when the federal government seemed to have discovered a national antidote to the Niger Delta militancy in its recent military expenditures against some of the militants into their riverrine enclaves in the Escravos creeks in the Niger Delta, it granted amnesty. Adherents of this school would liken the federal government's policy stance at such times to that of the United States of America of not negotiating with terrorists – a policy which prepares their terrorists' minds for a loss, even before they engage in any venture. Under this paradigm, the federal government would descend heavily on the militants as saboteurs and "smoke them out" as President George Bush would do and the government would then use its immense power and authority at its disposal. From this state-centric viewpoint, the government would not have relented in its unrestricted military action against the militants as such option not only conforms to the right of the federal government to do so but, also, that she has a comparative military advantage in securing ultimate victory at the end of the day.

If it takes an American government to lose several hundred soldiers just to retain its pride from an alleged desecration, as in the Philippines invasion of 1854 at San Juan and the Operations Desert Storm in the Gulf of the 1990s among others, what sacrifice does it matter to the national army, in terms of men and material, for the federal government to engage the militants on a bare military encounter? From a games theoretical framework, the capture of a major militant would be speculated to mean a lot in infusing fear and instilling a thought of withdrawal on other militants and their sponsors alike. Most Nigerians are fearful, especially in the face of a federal government contest. In this circumstance, it would be seen as premature for the federal government to concede amnesty while it is yet to ascertain the gains and prospects of its recent military reprisal on the militants. This is not to ignore the fact that a direct military encounter would produce a mixed impact. On a socio-psychological parlance, early amnesty to the militants would perceive the militants (in fact their sponsors) as having capitulated – their boys are no longer going to face the books, their true motives may never be known, their ventures may never be destroyed and their orchestrating nexus (whether internal or external) may never be discovered. This would then be a victory in disguise for the militants' cohorts and sponsors who may overtly rally round calls for more federal presence in regional development efforts in the Niger Delta. Besides, the Niger Delta people's struggle for a more practical fiscal federalism (otherwise known as resource control) may have been further vindicated, though.

On the other hand, some uncertain results of this policy may include forcing the militants to submission, destroying innocent lives of the local citizens, engaging in an endless battle that may incur the sponsorship of foreign state and or non-state adventurers, especially those who have stakes in the oil multinational companies operating in the region, in which case a Nigerian Nicaraguan would have emerged; and the destruction of the hard earned oil installations and investments of the federal government, among others. From this school of thought, no individual or group, no matter how highly placed, can be bigger or look intimidating to government. Adherents of state-centricism would embrace this option using the guise that the state has a duty to perform in the maintenance of social political continuity, stability and order.

The second school of thought would view the policy from a win-win theoretical standpoint and dispose the issue on a framework that sees the adoption of the amnesty policy as being borne out of government's tacit acceptance or desire to rethink its prevailing and, perhaps, indifferent policy towards the development of the Niger Delta region by virtue of its prevailing budgetary commitments in that direction. Adherents of this school of thought would praise the federal government for taking a bold and unusual step in initiating a peace overture to the militants in averting further trouble in the region by not choosing a full scale military option, which is quite against what statists would claim an abandonment of its key national security obligations with its uncertain results. It is already an over-romanticised fact in Nigeria that the quantum of development-oriented policies of the federal government towards the Niger Delta region, regarded as the geese that lay the golden egg in the Nigerian economy, falls far behind its commitments to exploitation and exploration of resources from the area.

There is a popular saying in the Niger Delta that 'Warri is the oil field while Abuja is the oil city'. This is an epitome of the impression of the Niger Delta peoples towards policy makers at Abuja, a place supposedly transformed into a mega city by the oil wealth of the Niger Delta – an insinuating paradox of development. To hurriedly prevent a total dismantling of the economic nerves of the country, planted in the Niger Delta region, the amnesty may have been contemplated as a panacea for staunching further damage to the economy in these trying times of global economic meltdown. Another, perhaps more lucid explanation under this school of thought, is that the amnesty option may have been selected in order for the Yar'Adua government to scuttle the ambitions of some probable unseen political adventurers of the region who may be using the militancy as their strategic political and economic launch pads for their bid towards the 2011 elections.

From whatever school of thought one views the issue, a major question here should be that of how profound and long lasting the seeming regional peace would be in the post-amnesty period and how committed would the federal government packages to the Niger Delta peoples be in the period of the administration of the policy. The amnesty period is for 60 days in the first instance during which all militant groups are expected to hand over their arms and ammunitions to the Nigerian government security officials at designated locations and centres. This process is also expected to be accompanied by a rehabilitation and pacification phase for the erstwhile militants for which some billions of naira has been earmarked in its administration.

The subtlety in this amnesty policy is that while the concession of amnesty to the Niger Delta militants may be seen from one school of thought as a reneging of the federal government in the use of its limitless state power in the exercise of its expected normal security obligations, it also implies that the militants would, by this policy, have no other option than to embrace peace in the region for the amnesty policy to take effect. However, the guarantee that the latter objective would be met is yet very edgy. Some of the relevant policy implications of the foregoing policy on the political economy of Nigeria can be identified:

1. The application of the amnesty policy would restore, albeit temporarily or permanently, a regional peace in the area. For while the militant activities lasted, illegal economic activities such as oil bunkering – illegal siphoning and sales of crude or its products into unauthorised trawlers – refining and distribution were going on simultaneously in form of informal "camps" amongst the militants such that, there were inter-camp clashes and misunderstandings. Should the militants or their sponsors devise another strategy in this respect, the federal government would then be justified to apply its strict military sanctions against the offenders. The envisaged peace would then rekindle normal life to the national economy and the oil companies would then go back to work again.

2. The renewed and unavoidable commitment of the federal government towards making manifest efforts in developing the Niger Delta is seriously implied in this amnesty policy. If it intends to reconcile the seemingly irreconcilable status of the nationalists and the ethnic politicians referred to earlier in this analysis, the federal government must go beyond just letters in making the minority Niger Delta people believe that they are

not being exploited by the nationalistic majority in the Nigerian political economy and democratisation process.

3. The amnesty policy would have truncated the economic and political ambitions of some of the adventurers in the militancy game who may, for implicit reasons of being charged for criminality, not show up in making any demands during the administration of the amnesty policy. This is perhaps one of the greatest praiseworthy points the federal government may have indirectly scored in adoption of the amnesty policy. For long, the suspicion that these militants have been operating at the instance of some unknown Niger Delta bigwigs has been profound in the Nigerian polity.

## 10.5. Conclusion

The adoption of the amnesty policy by the federal government on the Niger Delta militancy may have provided a short cut to the lingering economic crises created by the Niger Delta crisis on the Nigerian economy. Subject to a proper administration and a comprehensive consultative approach in its implementation, the amnesty policy for the Niger Delta militants would become one of Nigeria's most advised policy alternatives in recent time in resolving politico-economic conflict in the nation and an antidote to future crises of this objective and territorial dimension.

## 10.6. References

Atofarati, A.A. (1992) *The Nigerian Civil War, Causes, strategies and lessons learnt*, retrieved from the web http://www.africamasterweb.com/BiafranWarCauses.html

Cocktail, C. (2006) A conversation with Cuauhtémoc Cárdenas, *US Berkeley News*, March 23

Dinneya, G. (2006) *Political economy of democratization in Nigeria*, Lagos, Concept Publication Limited, P.39.

Imobighe, J. A.(2002) Warri crisis in historical and contemporary perspectives In J.A.Imobighe, C.O.Bassey & J.B.Asuni (Eds.) *Conflict and instability in the Niger Delta*, A publication of Academic Associates Peace Works, Ibadan, Spectrum Books Limited, Pp. 36-51.

US Immigration Amnesty (2009) Immigration*Amnesty*, http://www.usamnesty. org/

Ignatius Adeh

# Corruption and Environmental Law

The Case of the Niger Delta

African Politics/Politiques Africaines  Vol. 2

LIT

PATRICK ODIONIKHERE

# BRINGING DOWN THIS HOUSE

African Politics/Politiques Africaines          LIT

Ignatius Adeh
**Corruption and Environmental Law**
The Case of the Niger Delta
Dr. Adeh's work is a rich contribution to the discourse on oil resources and the twin problems of corruption and ecological degradation in Nigeria with lessons for other sub-Saharan African countries. It is indeed a purposeful scientific work on a theme of substantial contemporary interest, both practical and theoretical. Prof. Dr. Tesfatsion Medhanie He presents a compelling case on how to dethrone both problems of corruption and environmental degradation and enthrone a lasting sustainable development in the Niger Delta. The analysis of the problems is very objective and unbiased. A must read book for all. Hon.E. Ibeshi
Bd. 2, 2010, 408 S., 34,90 €, br., ISBN 978-3-643-10541-7

Patrick Odionikhere
**Bringing down this house**
For freedom to have a meaning, it must come through the sacrifice of the people. It is on this notion that the book narrates the journey of Nigeria and its people from the colonial perspective; it highlights contemporary realities with critical thoughts and gives an in-depth understanding of power politics. The book is a thorough work on Nigeria's historical and political evolution since the inception of its self-rule, with special appraisal on its political leaders. It provides insight on how Nigeria can be re-shaped by a new definition of power. The author argues persuasively, the road that should be taken by the people of Nigeria, in restoring the meaning of citizenship.
Bd. 1, 2008, 176 S., 19,90 €, br., ISBN 978-3-8258-1847-0

LIT Verlag Berlin – Münster – Wien – Zürich – London
Auslieferung Deutschland / Österreich / Schweiz: siehe Impressumsseite